Andrzej Przyłębski

Ethics in the Light of Hermeneutical Philosophy

Andrzej Przyłębski

Ethics in the Light of Hermeneutical Philosophy

Morality between (Self-)Reflection and Social Obligations

LIT

This book is printed on acid-free paper.

Bibliographic information published by the Deutsche Nationalbibliothek
The Deutsche Nationalbibliothek lists this publication in the Deutsche Nationalbibliografie; detailed bibliographic data are available on the Internet at http://dnb.d-nb.de.

ISBN 978-3-643-90897-1

A catalogue record for this book is available from the British Library

Klosbachstr. 107
CH-8032 Zürich
Tel. +41 (0) 44-251 75 05
E-Mail: zuerich@lit-verlag.ch http://www.lit-verlag.ch
Distribution:
In the UK: Global Book Marketing, e-mail: mo@centralbooks.com
In North America: International Specialized Book Services, e-mail: orders@isbs.com
In Germany: LIT Verlag Fresnostr. 2, D-48159 Münster
Tel. +49 (0) 2 51-620 32 22, Fax +49 (0) 2 51-922 60 99, e-mail: vertrieb@lit-verlag.de
In Austria: Medienlogistik Pichler-ÖBZ, e-mail: mlo@medien-logistik.at
e-books are available at www.litwebshop.de

For my wife Julia with love

Contents

Introduction

It might seem that ethics and hermeneutics are two separate philosophical disciplines, situated side by side though lacking an internal connection, within the particular whole that European philosophy constitutes. Yet the matter becomes somewhat more complicated when we realise that ethics, and on a broader plane practical philosophy, constitutes – next to theoretical philosophy and aesthetics – an element of the fundamental triad of philosophical disciplines that achieved stability following Kant and his three *Critiques*. When we treat hermeneutics purely as the theory and art of interpretation, its relationship with ethics remains purely external, technical, relating on the one hand to the cognitive effectiveness of a reading of the classic works in ethics, and on the other – to certain ethical indications regarding the reliability of comprehension and interpretation in general. The situation appears differently when by hermeneutics we understand hermeneutic philosophy not only as a certain manner of practising philosophy, but also as a certain set of convictions or views constituted during the development of this philosophical direction in the 20th century. Hermeneutics may then prove a valuable indicatorof how to practice ethical reflection in a modern manner. This may prove particularly valuable in the face of the evident crisis that philosophical ethics has fallen into.

This crisis is visible in the never-ending debates and new proposals and solutions occasionally resulting from them, ones that nobody takes seriously, i.e. as indicators for shaping one's own moral life. Although this could be understood as philosophical ethics' renouncement of being normative ethics, and its definitive shift to metaethical positions: the analyses of ethical judgments and motivations, etc., this would seem to signify a major and unforgiveable impoverishment, disqualifying – or at least weakening – philosophical ethics in confrontation with religiously motivated ethics. And nobody needs convincing today that such a confrontation, in the day of globalisation and the growing atheisation of European societies, must occur.

In his statement that "there are no moral facts, only moral interpretations of facts," Friedrich Nietzsche expressed not just his amoralism, only partly deriving from his disgust in the morality of his era and – as a consequence of the latter – from his will to reassess all values. This is because that amoralism could be treated as an individualistic extravagance of an eccentric thinker, striving at all costs to shed all those constraining obligations towards the society in which he had come to live. Quite another consequence of that statement, based on recognition of the interpretative character of morality, seems of much greater import. The provocative remark by the author of *Thus Spoke Zarathustra* thereby discloses the hermeneutic formation of the phenomenon of morality as such, meaning its dependence on the adoption of a certain attitude, a set of preliminary assumptions or convictions, which hermeneutic philosophy has tended to define as the prestructure of understanding since the publication of Martin Heidegger's *Being and Time.*

Hermeneutic philosophy bears a certain understanding of existence and knowledge. Existence emerges in the medium of signs (languageness) within the interpretative practices of human cultural communities. It is in them that objectivity appears, constituting in its essence no more than intersubjectivity. This is laid open brilliantly by the notion of "styles of thinking" developed by the brilliant Polish philosopher Ludwik Fleck. Hermeneutic philosophy is also a certain theory of knowledge – if only in the sense that it makes understanding (deriving from the life need to understand one's surrounding reality, the world in which one lives) the starting point for cognitive processes, initially those related to common sense, and later philosophical and specialist, scientific processes. Understanding is the starting point and destination for reasons unveiled by Heidegger, acknowledging *Dasein*, the conscious existence, as the *Worum-willen der Bedeutungszusammenhänge* ("for-the-sake-of-which" of semantic connections) – the centre of its "world," the source of its sense. Such hermeneutic epistemology is historicistic, but not relativistic, as its point of reference always constitutes the stabilised knowledge predominant in a particular life community (the ideal border of which is civilised humanity – Jürgen Habermas's *ideale Diskursgemeinschaft*).

The hermeneutic turn in philosophy that occurred in the latter half of the 20th century is something we owe not only to such thinkers as Wilhelm Dilthey, Heidegger, Hans-Georg Gadamer and Paul Ricoeur, who "as a standard" are classed among the founding fathers of the direction defined by the term "hermeneutic philosophy." A significant and even unavoidable contribution was made by such philosophers as Ernst Cassirer, Ludwig Wittgenstein and Habermas, rarely associated with this current. It was thanks to all the above that this turn became obvious, although it is not always thus defined. One speaks in this context of a *linguistic turn*, of an interpretationist, semiotic and even iconic turn. All these, I firmly believe, constitute a certain version of the hermeneutic turn in European philosophy.

This turn – which I have strived to show in many of my publications, in particular in the book *Hermeneutyczny zwrot filozofii* (Hermeneutic Turn of Philosophy, Wyd. Naukowe UAM, Poznan 2005) – led to far-reaching reassessments of European philosophy, and one could say to a certain shift in the thought paradigm. Characteristic features of the new style of thinking about philosophy are: (1) a rejection of metaphysics (in the traditional meaning of this term); (2) the questioning of the epistemological function of philosophy as purportedly constitutive for its contemporary functioning; and (3) acknowledging analysis of human existence in the world as such a task, as one determined by contingency (historicity, corporeality) and by understanding and interpretation.[1]

The relationship between hermeneutic philosophy and Nietzsche is characterised by a certain ambivalence. On the one hand, due to the salience of the interpretative character of man's relation with the surrounding reality, there is an appreciation of him as the pioneer of hermeneutic way of thinking about it. Yet on the other hand even his greatest admirers in the hermeneutists' camp do not share his occasionally extreme views regarding culture, truth, interpretation or morality (not to mention his absurd attacks on Christianity). However, one cannot remain indifferent to his sacrilegious ascertainment of the "death of God," because despite all its simplifications it indicates a significant change that transpired in European societies over the past two centuries, and it is sometimes called the end of metaphysics, the exhausting of the power and significance of the great narratives, narratives that from time to time led to totalitarian ideologies but that were also worldviews regulating the lives of entire civilisations. There is evidently a crisis in ethics. This is visible if only in the growing demand for experts and the mushrooming of diverse occupational ethics, striving to regulate something once regulated by an ordinary sense of decency, rooted in the ethical awareness of practically every person.

It comes as no surprise, therefore, that this provoked me to raise the question of how ethics practised from a hermeneutic perspective looks and how it could look. The first part of the answer to this question is contained in this book. It is the first part because – starting with Heidegger's undoubtedly correct assertion that there is no systematic philosophy without a history of philosophy, but neither is there any point in practising the history of philosophy

[1] I omit here possible further attributes of hermeneutic philosophy (e.g. the linguality of understanding, proposed by Gadamer), as they are not accepted by all those representing this direction.

devoid of questions deriving from active philosophising – I began my research into the relationship between hermeneutics and ethics with an analysis of the contemplations by the classics of hermeneutic philosophy: Schleiermacher, Dilthey, Heidegger, Gadamer and Ricoeur. I added to this an analysis of the ethical concept put forward by interpretationism, a theory – in my firm opinion – not only close to hermeneutic philosophy but also one expanding upon numerous threads of the latter in a creative and discursive manner.

A little surprisingly, this has proved an area of interesting discoveries. Whereas the significance of ethical research for Ricoeur was – in the light of his last works published just before his death – obvious and widely known, as also known was the discussion regarding whether the fundamental ontology presented by Heidegger in *Sein und Zeit* was simultaneously fundamental ethics, and whereas certain people know Gadamer's somewhat puzzling assertion that his concept really belongs to practical and not theoretical philosophy, the discovery of the fundamental significance of ethics in Schleiermacher's all-encompassing philosophical concept struck me as somewhat surprising. In most treatises regarding this philosopher, this thread is bypassed due to the position gained by his dialectics and hermeneutics. An even greater surprise was the discovery of Dilthey's ethical considerations. Their omission by authors of monographies on this particular philosopher is justified, since Dilthey never chose to announce them in print. They seemed sufficiently important and original to me that I decided to present and to analyse them.

A presentation of the ethical concepts of the classics of hermeneutic thinking comprises the content of the first six chapters of this book. However, it is the final chapter that constitutes its crowning and, at the same time, its purpose. This is because the question that guided my explorations was of a systematic nature, and may be worded as comprising two equally important parts:

1. What is morality, what kind of character does its validity have if we acknowledge its fundamentally interpretative nature, and how is it situated on the map of symbolic compositions and constructs demarcating the azimuths of our spiritual world, the world of our lives. This question entails a subsequent one: will an ethical stance, due to the virtualisation of our existence in the world as endorsed by postmodernism, soon become a relic of the past, perhaps something beautiful but at the same time obsolete and rare, and perhaps even an expression of weakness of those who adopt it, of their excessive traditionalism, and *ergo* something the disappearance of which – e.g. in favour of the exclusiveness of legislation – is preordained?

2. What is ethics, especially philosophical ethics, i.e. what is the status and what is the power of analyses of morality and ethical indications evolved laboriously in ever more subtle treatises by philosophers specialising in this

sub-discipline? This also signifies the following question: does the philosopher-ethicist here have the status of an expert, whose knowledge surpasses the ethical facility of the ordinary mortal and thereby guarantees him a "higher ethicality," and if so, then in what sense?

It was for these systematic reasons that I opted against carrying out a reconstruction of the ethical concepts of a few unquestionably important thinkers sometimes linked to the term "hermeneutics" in the main section. I have in mind here for example the transcendental pragmatism of Karl-Otto Apel, the philosophy of "weak existence" and "weak thought" formed for years by Gianni Vattimo, or the neo-pragmatism of Richard Rorty. Their hermeneutic affiliations are well known, and their ethical insights may also prove momentous and useful in the future. However, none of them are among the classics in this field, and even more so because in their concepts they combine hermeneutic threads with elements alien to this philosophy (transcendentalism in the case of Apel, nihilism and deconstruction in the case of Vattimo, and pragmatism in the case of Rorty). As such their inclusion in the project of hermeneutical ethics has temporarily been set aside for further research which is undoubtedly essential here.

The phrase "hermeneutical ethics" used a moment ago is by no means here by accident. The intention of creating prolegomena for a hermeneutical depiction of morality has motivated my research since the beginning. This book, as has already been said, is a summary of its first stage. Hermeneutic philosophy, despite inflation of the term "hermeneutics" that we are currently dealing with, has made irreversible reassessments in western philosophy. Above all it has pushed practical philosophy into the foreground as the most important task today, which is meant to shoulder the now 25-century venture called philosophy. Hermeneutic philosophy – and this is also the main tendency of the concepts presented here – has also questioned thinking of practical philosophy in categories of "pure theory," i.e. theory in the style of the natural sciences, the application of which is conditioned by the desire to accomplish the goals they may serve. Ethical research – it so happens – has an essentially different character. Here one cannot simply point out to others the path one is not taking oneself, and yet retaining one's credibility. This opens us to such an understanding of the phenomenon of morality and ethicality that binds its existence to our concern, our self-formation and also vigilance, the purpose of which is its protection and development.

* * *

At this point I would like to express my sincere gratitude to those who, through their support, have contributed to the fruition of this book. I have in mind here my German friends, Prof. Ferdinand Fellmann and Prof. Günter Abel, with whom discussions regarding ethical-hermeneutical issues moved my research forward; my wife Julia, who strived to ensure the best possible conditions for writing, and the Minister of Science and Higher Education, whose financial support enabled access to the latest literature and essential consultation.

Chapter 1

Ethics According to Schleiermacher

Friedrich Daniel Ernst Schleiermacher (1768-1834) is quite rightly considered an outstanding hermeneutist and theoretician of hermeneutics, and many – this author among them – also appreciate his contribution to the emergence of hermeneutic philosophy, conceived as a certain new philosophical standpoint.[1] Much less well known is the fact that Schleiermacher also created his own, original ethical standpoint. For him ethics was – perhaps surprisingly – even more important than hermeneutics, as it established intellectual boundaries within which hermeneutics could properly function (as the art and theory of interpretation) as well as the critique coupled with it. "Hermeneutics and Critique" – it is this conceptual pair that distinguishes the hermeneutic thought of this philosopher, theologian and translator of Berlin.[2]

Much research and many treatises have been dedicated – in Poland as well – to Schleiermacher's hermeneutic theory, based on the one hand on posing the transcendental question of "how is (intersubjectively important) understanding possible?," and on the other on analysis of his own hermeneutic practice as a translator and preacher.[3] As such it is high time to present if only an outline of the ethics developed by this philosopher, one it would be

[1] In my book *Hermeneutyczny zwrot filozofii* [Hermeneutic Turn of Philosophy], Wyd. Naukowe UAM, Poznan 2005), this important thinker is covered by Chapter 3: *Schleiermachera hermeneutyczne przezwyciężenie idealizmu* (pp. 57-78).

[2] Schleiermacher's treatise under just such a title (*Hermeneutik und Kritik, mit besonderer Beziehung auf Neues Testament*) was published in 1838 in Berlin by his student Frierdich Lücke. Its critical edition was published by Frankfurt's Suhrkamp Verlag.

[3] Suffice to mention the works of Maciej Potępa, particularly *Dialektyka i hermeneutyka w filozofii F.D. Schleiernachera* [Dialectics and Hermeneutics in the Philosophy of F.D. Schleiermacher], Wyd. Uniwersytetu Łódzkiego, Łódź 1992.

no exaggeration to place alongside such philosophers as Fichte, Schelling or even Hegel.

Born in 1768, Schleiermacher remained under the influence of pietism up until he commenced studies in Halle in 1787. His studies opened his eyes to the power, wealth and innovativeness of the ideas of the Enlightenment.His attention was drawn from the start of this spiritual transformation particularly by practical philosophy. He devoted his first treatise, still as a student, to commenting on Aristotle's theory of friendship, contemplated in *Nicomachean Ethics.* In these years of his youth he also diligently studied Kant's *Critique of Practical Reason.* Much of his six-hundred-page-strong first volume of his *Works* (published from 1980 by the DeGruyter Publishers) is dedicated to ethical issues. He retained his interest in practical philosophy throughout his life, on eight occasions delivering a series of lectures on ethics at university, which he planned to have printed. It was ethics that was supposed to constitute the trunk of the tree whose branches, in his opinion, were aesthetics, hermeneutics, the philosophy of religion, philosophy of the state, pedagogics and the science of history.

His early fascination with the ethics of Aristotle meant that Schleiermacher was unable to acknowledge Kant's concept as an adequate grasp of the theory of morality. His opposition to the ethical theory predominant then in Germany can be seen notably in his treatises of 1788-1793, the spirit of which he remained faithful to until the end of his days. The sole thing he desired to adopt from Kant was the rational development of ethical theory according to "strictly scientific method."

As the starting point and perhaps even a type of azimuth of his ethical deliberations, Schleiermacher takes not *a priori*moral law, butthe highest good, which he understands as the entirety of what is ethical (*Sittlichkeit*). Initially he understands this as a pure, regulative principle, but shortly (and ultimately) he links it to "materially fulfilled ethicality," which is achieved in the historical process. He also immediately challenges the rigorism of Kant's formalistic ethics, subjugating the individual to *a priori* moral law. According to the author of *Hermeneutik und Kritik*, the ethicality of human action derives not only from the general laws of reason, but also from individual self-discovery, from recognising one's own essence. He maintains that the meaningfulness of the social institution that morality constitutes is decided by the possibility of reconciling what is shared with what is individual – "harmonious equilibrium between tendencies that serve the good of the community and tendencies aimed towards achieving individual interests."[4] Schleiermacher appears to believe that Kant

[4] Such a claim is contained in the monography on Schleiermacher by his most outstanding expert today, Gunter Scholtz (*Ethik und Hermeneutik. Schleiermachers Grundlegung der Wissenschaften*, Suhrkamp Verlag, Frankfurt am Main 1995, p. 25) [transl. from the Polish – J. Weber].

is tearing apart the connection of what exists with what should exist, which transforms practical philosophy into a utopian venture.In his opposition to this, the Berlin theologian declares that "if we cannot what we should, and if we do not know that we can," then the binding character of ethical norms becomes but a chimera.[5]

That discovering oneself becomes recognised as an essential element of ethicality constitutes a significant *novum* in relation to Kant's concept then prevailing. The opposition of universal moral right and the individual subjugated to this, consumed by passions, undergoes yet stronger questioning through the emphasis – citing Aristotle – of the significance of friendship and companionship, and thus an individual's relationships with select Others and with mediocre Others. This thread is picked up – as we shall see in one of the later chapters – by the French philosopher Paul Ricoeur, whose triad of being-oneself, care-for-another and justice-for-all shall become the foundation of reflection over the phenomenon of ethicality in its entirety.

However, the most powerful anti-Kantian overtone may, it would seem, lie in Schleiermacher's rejection of the main principle upon which Kant's ethics is based: his "fact of freedom" (in noumenal order, i.e. as the possibility of reason beginning a totally undetermined chain of new events). Schleiermacher is sceptical of the dualism of natural determinism *versus* ethical freedom (non-determination). He believes that freedom thus understood not only clashes with the principles of empirical psychology, but also "carries" a personal identity (a so-called unity) as the relative permanence of the ethical character on which an individual may work, precisely because there exists a psychological causality. The existence of freedom in the sense postulated by Kant would lead to the invalidation of this possibility. Schleiermacher opines that moral law may only be effective when it is capable of defining (stimulating) a feeling, while this determines will, and a consequence of this is action, which can be termed ethical. Apart from physical forces there also exist psychic forces, which do not differ from the former in any fundamental way. The adoption of totally free will, independent of psychic processes, would cast man from the real world.

In this approach as well the thinking of Aristotle "shines through"; for him, ethicality did not derive from decisions taken by totally free will, but from the habits the ethical character of a given individual had, properly developed and nurtured. Free will was not, in this portrayal, a condition *sine qua non*of ethical attitudes and deeds. Advocating such an understanding is particularly unusual as we have to bear in mind that Schleiermacher was a Protestant theologian. Therefore, in order not to fall into conflict with the doctrine of

[5] F.D.E. Schleiermacher, *Kritische Gesamtausgabe*, Walter de Gruter, Berlin – New York 1980 et seq. (cited later as KGA), vol. 1, pt. 1, p. 221 [transl. from the Polish – J. Weber].

his Church, he carefully separates his contemplations regarding morality from his research related to the philosophy of religion. On the one hand the main purpose of religion is not, in his opinion – and as opposed to the opinions of Kant or Hegel[6] – of an ethical nature, while on the other ethics should not allow itself to be absorbed by the philosophy of religion. Which is not to say that subjective motivation for taking an ethical stance cannot derive from a religious stance. What it means is only that religion does not possess an ethics-consolidating function. Moral awareness should stick to this – and not that – world, i.e. to the finished real world. To cite Gunter Scholtz, such an approach may be defined as a position of immanence.[7] This German scholar states: "And so the young Schleiermacher, interested almost exclusively in philosophical ethics up until 1793, takes elements of pre-Kantian ethics, exposes them independently and evolves them critically against Kantianism, despite it serving as a scientific gauge for him. And these elements are: the notion of the highest good as the totality (*Inbegriff*) of material ethicality, an attempt at creating an equilibrium between the general ethical norm and the individuality of man as a complete being, avoidance of the dualism of nature and freedom, and separating religion and theology from ethical action and philosophical ethics."[8]

In 1803 Schleiermacher writes his work *Outlines of a Critique of the Doctrines of Morality to date,* containing the fundamental components of his future system of ethics. Its centre comprises learning about the highest good as the totality of all goods understood as cultural or community goods. These include state, church, companionship, family, and research community. Ethicality understood as just such a wholeness is achieved in the historical process. As a result, ethics becomes the theory of human culture and history.[9]

Schleiermacher sets his ethical theory the task of joining the theory of goods with the theory of virtues and moral duties. It is therefore supposed to connect ancient ethics, as the science of being ethical (of a "good" life), with modern ethics, understood as the science of moral obligation. Thanks to this approach Schleiermacher not only combines but also mediates between what is individual and what is general. General goods, such as state or family, are the result of individuals' ethically valuable actions and behaviours. Their existence in turn produces moral content, establishes a certain kind of materially fulfilled ethical framework for individuals' behaviours. What is general does

[6] Cf. Z. Kuderowicz, *Kant*, Wiedza Powszechna, Warsaw 2000, pp. 94-100 (chapters: "Religia rozumu" and "Umoralniająca rola religii").

[7] Cf. G. Scholtz, *Ethik und Hermeneutik...*, op. cit., p. 26.

[8] Ibidem, p. 27.

[9] F.D.E. Schleiermacher, *Ethik (1812/1813),* Meiner Verlag, Hamburg 1990, pp. 8 and 203-204.

not exist without the human individuals maintaining its existence, while they draw the guidelines for their thinking and behaviour from the existence of general goods, of community goods.

Ethical theory thus constructed evidently departs from ethics understood exclusively from the direction of moral norms (binding for the individual), and becomes a theory of concrete ethicality (in the sense of "morality," signalised after all in the German word *Sitte*, the source of the term *Sittlichkeit*), understood as the substance (in Hegel's meaning of this word) of human culture developed in history. One should note that this is a deeply hermeneutic depiction, in keeping with the hermeneutic philosophy created by Gadamer, and his concept of historical reason.[10]

However, the consequences of such a measure are astounding. And this is because ethics thus unexpectedly becomes a universal theory of the human world (i.e. of culture as historically understood), which makes it possible to present it as a framework theory for all of the humanities and social sciences, and setting them against the natural sciences (Aristotle's "physics"). What is real (nature) and what is ideal (reason) are represented as the two fundamental and different manifestations of the Absolute (Existence). This does not mean, however, the complete divergence of these two spheres of existence, since reason individualises and crystallises in the historical process, and when combining with nature – which it needs to accomplish its goals – it constitutes a new unity of what is real and what is ideal. That historical process is thereby an ethical process.[11]

It is impossible not to notice the similarities between these ideas and what emerges later in Hegel's work. However, there are also significant differences between them, differences which we shall lend more clarity to later. For now it is important to realise that in attacking Kant's position (and also Fichte's), and reducing morality to a principle taking the form of a moral law meant to curtail the nature (in man) threatening ethicality, Schleiermacher establishes the foundations for the hermeneutic idea of "formative ethics" in the individual, shaping their capability and strength essential for filling the culture that created it with ethical content. At the same time this filling signifies the crystallisation of ethicality. Schleiermacher's ethics therefore does not create general principles or rules, but rather shows the prospect of ethicality, which – at least in part – is an element of the cultural reality in which man lives and functions.

However, Schleiermacher's ethical theory is considered so broadly, that it becomes not only a theory of culture, but also a theory of society. Although it draws its significant sources mainly – though not only – from ancient

[10] Cf. A. Przyłębski, *Hermeneutyczny zwrot...*, op. cit., pp. 154-190.

[11] F.D.E. Schleiermacher, *Ethik (1812/1813)*, pp. 11 et seq.

philosophy (some researchers maintain that more from Plato than Aristotle, although that would seem to be going too far), when taking a closer look one cannot but notice that – as with Hegel – it is a theory of modern society. This is because one can see in it an evident break from the hierarchical side of the traditional stratified society, while the structure that emerges in Schleiermacher's deductions is of an organic character, the equally important conditioning of all components, and not a metaphysical structure based on the tree metaphor (roots, trunk and branches), introduced by Descartes and sometimes used by Schleiermacher.[12]

One could even risk the assertion that Schleiermacher's thinking is somewhat more modern than Hegel's, as he rejects not only the metaphorical understanding of the spirit, replacing it with a consistently used understanding of (human) reason, but also Hegel's hierarchy of spirituality: from the subjective, via the objective and to the absolute spirit. Among other things, this signifies a questioning of the superiority of philosophy (as the highest form of theoretical life) over art or religion; the same applies to the (alleged) superiority of the state (state life) over a self-fulfilling individual or family (family life).[13]

Nevertheless, it has to be added that in Schleiermacher's concept as well, freedom plays a fundamental role, although not – as understood by Kant – as an ahistorical "fact of freedom," distinguishing every rational being, but as the historically conditioned possibility of human self-fulfilment, assuming varied form in different eras and in different societies. Only developed culture gives man the full possibility of achieving freedom, meaning – oneself as a free existence. Such culture is described by Schleiermacher from an ethical point of view (in his understanding of ethics), meaning as a certain structure of goods, the whole (entirety) of which constitutes that "highest good." According to him, the ideal of humanity is not – as for example according to Schiller or Nietzsche – the creative life of an artist (self-fulfilment in the area of aesthetics), but participation in all types of good appropriate for the individual predispositions of every human individual.

This system of goods, demarcating the structure of a developed society, is defined via the need (or value) of identity, characterised on the one hand by the need to belong (homogeneity, unanimity with somebody in relation to something), and on the other by the need for difference (otherness, retaining one's individualness). These two complementary needs, jointly creating individual identity, are fulfilled in two separate but interconnected areas: (a) in the area of guaranteeing existential foundations via the mastering – thanks to the organisation of collective life – of nature, and (b) through the expression

[12] Cf. R. Descartes, *Zasady filozofii*, transl. I. Dąmbska, PWN, Warsaw 1960, p. 367.

[13] Cf. F.D.E. Schleiermacher, *Ethik (1812/1813)*, p. 87 et seq.

of individual spiritual needs in the form of symbolic activeness, in regard to cultural life. The first aspect expresses the organisational side, and the second aspect – the expressive side of existence of human community. Let us leave aside the problematic question of how organisational activity is possible without cognitive activity, which Schleiermacher places among the expressive functions. Let us limit ourselves here to only giving examples that will facilitate comprehension of the goods' structure as created by the Berlin hermeneutist. And so the need for belonging is fulfilled in the sphere of organisation by the state and law, and in the sphere of symbolisation (expression) – by learning (led by academia, the highest manifestation of knowledge community). However, the need for differentiation or for retaining otherness is fulfilled in the area of organisation by "unrestrained sociability," manifested in how one runs one's home (and in participation in social life), whilst in the sphere of symbolisation its fulfilment is ensured (or at least enabled) by religion and art.

It is with this structure and its related ideal of humanity that Schleiermacher distances himself – in a way similar to how Hegel does it – from the romanticist pipe dreams of a return to homogenous culture modelled on the Middle Ages, reacting at the same time to the diversification of modern society as a result of the development of division of work – the *signum temporis* of the age in which he had come to live.

In addition the absence of hierarchicalism in the structuring of the individual areas of the goods also shows that Schleiermacher noticed and positively assessed the idea of emancipation for specific areas of culture and the related new areas of man's creative and unconstrained self-fulfilment. On the other hand, he strived to protect this construct from disintegrating into autonomic and disconnected spheres by attempting to show that they are a function and product of one and the same reason. The task of his ethical theory is therefore to integrate diverse manifestations of human life by placing them within the whole that culture constitutes. Because this is the "highest good," the individual should feel obliged to protect it through active participation in it. And this is a rare case in Schleiermacher's ethical thinking of the formulation of a certain norm, because his ethics is more descriptive in character than normative. Which does not mean that by unveiling to the individual the new areas of freedom historically emerging they are not made aware of the responsibility that lands on their shoulders for upholding and developing culture as an environment of truly human life.

One could say that Schleiermacher is more hermeneutic here than Hegel in the way he proceeds: he rejects superhuman automatism of the spirit, and acknowledging the symbolic (i.e. interpretative) character of culture strives to make individuals aware of their role in maintaining its existence: responsibility both for raising it to a higher level and for its decline. Schleiermacher's attitude towards the state also seems more modern than Hegel's. Whereas the author of *The Phenomenology of Spirit* favours granting states a special place in the advancing awareness of freedom, Schleiermacher portrays the state as one of many instruments regulating culture as a whole. Overestimation of the role of the state in Hegel's political philosophy, evident if only in how it is treated as an absolute goal in itself,[14] constitutes for Schleiermacher a threat to individuals' unconstrained self-fulfilment, to their freedom.

According to Schleiermacher, the state is not a form of objective spirit or the highest good, but a social instrument that has two fundamental tasks: to manage society (mainly related to the organisation of economic life) and to retain the nation's existence within a given territory by sustaining armed forces (understood as defensive forces). These two functions should remain in an equilibrium; upsetting that leads either to the emergence of a militarised state in which the armed forces achieve an unjustified advantage, or the emergence of an excessively industrialised state in which the excessive interference by governmental institutions in economic matters upsets civic freedom.

As such, where Hegel perceives in the existence of a (powerful) state a guarantee of proper development of a given nation and its culture, Schleiermacher strives to reduce the state's omnipotence, seeing in its domination a threat to individual freedom and to the harmonious development of the culture of the nation as a whole. One could risk stating that for Schleiermacher the state is of only instrumental value and could be replaced by a different form organising this aspect of social life, while for Hegel it has intrinsic value – metaphysical and also substantial. This is because in the way in which a given state is organised not only is the condition of a particular society's spiritual development unveiled, but so too is its place in the hierarchically considered process of the growth of freedom, of mankind, and ultimately of the absolute spirit, which is achieved in the historical process.[15]

---

[14] Cf. e.g. comments by Georg Wilhelm Friedrich Hegel: 1. "The state is the actuality of the substantial *will* [...] it is the *rational* in and for itself. This substantial unity is an absolute and unmoved end in itself [...] in relation to individuals, whose *highest duty* is to be members of the state," and 2. "The states, nations, and individuals involved in this business of the world spirit emerge with their own *particular and determinate principle*, which has its interpretation and actuality in their *constitution* and throughout the whole *extent* of their *condition* [...] they are at the same time the unconscious instruments and organs of that inner activity in which the shapes which they themselves assume pass away, while the spirit in and for itself prepares and works its way towards the transition to its next and higher stage." G.W.F. Hegel, *Elements of the Philosophy of Right*, transl. H.B. Nisbet, Cambridge University Press, Cambridge2003, pp. 275 and 373.

[15] Cf. G.W.F. Hegel, *Wykłady z filozofii dziejów* [Lectures on the History of Philosophy], trans. J. Grabowski and A. Landman, PWN, Warsaw 1958.

This otherness in the portrayal, which – as needs emphasising – is differentiation within fundamental similarity, can also be seen in the assessment of family. Whereas Hegel places it on the first level of ethicality, assigning it the function of preparing the individual for living in a modern society, fundamental for the whole of ethicality, Schleiermacher grants the family (the family "home") a function that is independent of both state and of purely economic organisation of work, i.e. the function of civic society. For Schleiermacher the family home is something more than just preparation for living in a civic society or even a chance for a certain moral acculturation, i.e. the primal 'ethical programming' based on love and trust. It is for him above all the place for fulfilling human otherness, uniqueness, materialising both in the right to inviolability of the home from without and when in hospitality – in the right to lead one's social life in keeping with one's own preferences. "Unconstrained sociability" is what makes a particular home a place of self-fulfilment of ethicality, also due to the uninhibited respecting of conventions that enable this exchange of ideas, appraisements and values, exchange that develops the individual. The exchange of ideas insubordinate to instrumental thinking, "unconstrained conversation" as Schleiermacher calls it, belongs in his opinion to creative, artistic thinking. It is therefore part of something that, citing Hegel, may be reflected by the word *Bildung*, signifying education combined with formation. With the only difference being that whereas for Hegel individual formation (shaping "subjectivity" in its specificity) is an interim phase towards grasping what is general, towards evolving oneself towards generality, for Schleiermacher it is a goal in itself: he perceives it as a chance for the realisation and articulation of differences (and not identity), which may lead to further development (differentiation and enrichment) of culture. This is achieved thanks to the richness concealed within the creative individual, but the condition for its materialisation is the institution of the family home, the embodiment of the spheres of privacy and sociability at the same time.[16]

The state and law on the one hand, and the home (unconstrained social life) on the other, fill Schleiermacher's perception of this sphere of human *praxis*, which is connected to the organisation of community life in order to survive in nature. Ethicality, connected to the institution of state, is determined by the state law in force, while the ethicality of social relations – by customary conventions. Is there room here – one could ask – for a truly unconstrained, individual ethical deed? A similar question could be addressed to the other side of the ethical construct created by Schleiermacher, a construct determined by scientific life (academia), religious life (the churches) and artistic life

[16] Cf. F.D.E. Schleiermacher, *Ethik (1812/1813)*, pp. 126 et seq.

(schools, areas of study). They are also ruled by convention, by custom, while the question regarding the place for authentic ethicality, i.e. the individual's consideration over the moral value of their deed, seems out of place here. This is so despite a certain advantage that Schleiermacher's concept has over Hegel's: whilst with Hegel the whole undoubtedly holds the advantage (meaning higher value) over the individual, Schleiermacher wishes to retain the equilibrium between them, treating them as two extremes of ethicality. This creates room for the individual's creativity, including in the area of transforming the prevailing morality. However, Schleiermacher (as well as Hegel, and that to a greater degree) is unable to conceptualise in his theory what such an attitude correcting a particular morality would be guided by. On the other hand Kant – whom they criticised – provided us with an appropriate tool in the form of the categorical imperative. *Also muss es zu Kant zurück gegangen werden*?[17] Perhaps. However, Kant should certainly be corrected by taking into consideration the justifiable criticism of his practical philosophy penned by Schleiermacher and Hegel, nineteenth-century restorers of ethical Aristotelianism.

Be that as it may, Schleiermacher (just like Hegel) turns out to be a theoretician of social ethics somewhat neglecting issues related to individual ethics. Moreover, he is inclined within this social ethics to idealise society, i.e. to perceive it in categories of an ethical community actually existing (a community of values and attitudes). Perhaps this was still, at least partially, justified in his day. But Max Weber showed that one hundred years later this assumption had ceased to be valid; the polytheism of values triumphant at the turn of the twentieth century made the possibility of society existing as an ethical community something of little credence.[18] From this point on the overall appraisal of a particular society as moral or immoral seems a misunderstanding.

Nevertheless, this does not change the need for an individual ethics. After all, man is unable to see himself as an anonymous puppet steered by the industrial, political and ideological forces of society, a person on whom nothing depends. Schleiermacher has less than Kant or Emmanuel Levinas to offer somebody facing ethical dilemmas, although that is not to say he has nothing

[17] In writing "Should one not therefore go back to Kant?" we are making a travesty of the well-known call by Otto Liebmann, pioneer of neo-Kantianism, from his book *Kant und die Epigonen* (Stuttgart 1865), each chapter of which ends in an appeal to go back to Kant as the source of dependable philosophy. Cf. in this matter Andrzej Przyłębski, *W poszukiwaniu królestwa filozofii. Z dziejów neokantyzmu badeńskiego*, Wyd. UAM, Poznan 1993.

[18] Cf. M. Weber, "'Duch' kapitalizmu" [The Protestant Ethic and the Spirit of Capitalism], in Z. Krasnodębski, *M. Weber*, Wiedza Powszechna, Warsaw 1999, pp. 148-169. An interesting (as hermeneutically mediated) defensive response to Weber's devastating arguments is contained in the writings of his Heidelberg friend Ernst Troeltsch (cf. E. Troeltsch, *Religia, kultura, filozofia*, transl. A. Przyłębski, Wyd. Poznańskie, Poznan 2006).

to offer. In the part of his ethics that talks of ethical merits, he emphasises for example the cardinal importance of consideration, wisdom, love and perseverance, and that in relation to all areas of social life. In addition, by acknowledging – in the character of a regulative ideal – unity in multiplicity, he proclaims the existence of a formal ethical principle independent of social differentiation. As Gunter Scholtz rightly states, his ethics also uses a certain philosophical criterion for appraising the ethicality of a particular human community. This is the degree of equilibrium between society and the individual. One could also agree with this German researcher when he claims that "the structure of the highest good takes on the role of formal ethical rights."[19] This is from where Schleiermacher draws his individual ethics – although indeed only as an outline. It comprises two parts: the knowledge of ethical benefits (virtues), and the knowledge of duties (obligations). Yet the whole time he bears in mind that ethical deeds (behaviours) should not only praise rational freedom, limiting itself by granting itself rights, but that their purpose is to maintain both the spiritual development of society and its culture as the essential frames within which man's humanity and his individual talents may be fulfilled.

Human individuals manifest something that Kant called "asocial sociability," and which Schleiermacher expresses as the presence of two tendencies in a person: the tendency to put down roots in a community, to generate something that he calls "the awareness of Us," and the tendency to articulate one's unique existence, which he described as "the awareness of Me." The ethical task of each individual is to not fall into either of these extremes, to hold them in relative equilibrium, in a kind of "homeostasis." This results in natural obligations imposed on the individual. The condition for their fulfilment to be possible is, in turn, the development – initially in the process of upbringing, and later in self-education based on own experience – of certain traits of character constituting ethical virtues. In reference to the classic theory of ethicality, Schleiermacher speaks in this context of prudence, justice, wisdom, respect, charity, and readiness to give help.

As for the duties that, according to Schleiermacher's ethical theory, befall the individual, they refer to the person's place (position) in society, and are tied to the communities in which one participates in different ways and to a varying degree. If starting from his fundamental ethical construct, one could accept that there are (at least) four such communities: public (participation in the life of the state, regulated by law), private (participation in social life, regulated by custom), religious (attitude towards church and religions) and scientific (attitude towards new knowledge). One could also add aesthetic communities to

[19] G. Scholtz, *Ethik und Hermeneutik...*, op. cit., p. 64.

this – the attitude towards works of art and to art in general. Because a healthy society means the harmonious development of them all, individuals have the obligation of contributing – appropriately to their capabilities – to this balanced development. As Scholtz, already cited above, rightly states: "The vision of ethicality that is drawn by the learnings of goods is becoming the norm for the ethical behaviour of individuals, because goods, and together with them the ethicality of societies, are only achieved through the duty and virtues of the people functioning there. This is why Schleiermacher's teachings about obligations and virtues relate in both content and structure to these goods."[20]

It is worth adding here that despite Schleiermacher's hermeneutics not yet being a fully-fledged hermeneutic philosophy, but at the most its embryo, his ethical reflection embraces it anyway. In his opinion hermeneutics is, above all, an auxiliary discipline, the fundamental task of which is to favour communication via the comprehension of sense conveyed. Appraisal of how this task is fulfilled also fits on the axis of moral – immoral. "The ethical gift of comprehension involves, according to Schleiermacher, the acknowledgement of a lingual utterance by Another as an utterance of reason, and not as a sound devoid of sense; and secondly on the acknowledgement of their individuality and otherness, which cannot be perceived as a shortcoming or something indifferent. These aspects must not be separated, as rhetoric (*Rede*) is individualised reason."[21]

Comprehending, as an action generating a community of equal partners to an agreement, is an activity that is ethical in character. This equality is manifested in Schleiermacher claiming that the first goal of understanding is to grasp the intended sense – unlike Gadamer, who talks of equal rights as "acknowledging as genuine." Only the next step, belonging not to hermeneutics but to criticism, is an assessment of its authenticity. Another ethical aspect of hermeneutic activeness is enabling another individual to have a say, i.e. such expansion of one's own interpretational horizons that does not press what is alien into what is one's own, but that broadens them, creating a new point of view. "To understand is to learn the Other's language."[22] However, this does not mean full identification or merging into one: Schleiermacher's well-known "understand the author better than he understood himself" is based on the interpreter, after understanding the author "equally as well as he himself," creating distance from which he can make an even deeper and broader appraisal of the meaning of what is to be interpreted (understood).

[20] Ibidem, p. 132.
[21] Ibidem, pp. 143-144.
[22] Ibidem, p. 145.

In summarising, it must be stated that Schleiermacher's ethics is at a similar level to Hegel's. It is a concept based on the morality and ethicality actually existing in every society (the famous *Sittlichkeit*, the equivalent of the Greek *ethos*). The individual is immersed in the culture that humanises them, makes them a person, grants them human dignity. This individual's rationality naturally plays a significant role here, although ethicality is not limited to rational verification of whether this individual's deed is in keeping with the a priori moral law. The point of reference here is the moral order prevailing in a specific society, containing norms that are clear to the individual consciously participating in this society's life. This is why this ethics does not strive to multiply the formal or material action guidelines. The fundamental differences between Schleiermacher and Hegel lies in the fact that Hegel's model is dynamic, evolutionary, that its two elements (the family and civic society) play in it the roles of a certain type of preparation for the coming into existence of a third element, i.e. the state, as the most complete fulfilment of the spirit (which also means the ethicality) of a particular nation.

Schleiermacher's model has the character of a structure in which all parts mutually condition one another, and as such the state does not play a distinguished role here. Overestimated, it may even function in an anti-ethical way, restricting individuals' liberty of life and expression, and the development of their creative individuality. The question regarding what to do in a situation of glaring conflicts of values may, in this approach, only be resolved by referring to the criterion of the good of society.Individual conscience here is significant only insofar as it is an expression (a voice) of the internalised hierarchy of values imposed on the individual through their participation in collective life.

The relative superiority of the hermeneutist Schleiermacher over the speculative idealist Hegel seems to lie mainly in the fact that in his concept the individual's rights to self-fulfilment are equally as important as the rights of culture to be as it is. What is more – Schleiermacher has the instruments for the critique of culture (*ergo* society) in which the equilibrium in relations between citizen and state would be distorted (destroyed) to the state's advantage: in the light of his ethics, a totalitarian state would have to be rejected just as would a society comprising scattered people not connected to one another in any way.

Chapter 2

Wilhelm Dilthey's Outline of Philosophical Ethics

Wilhelm Dilthey (1833-1911) is among the classic figures of hermeneutic theory and one of the leading creators of hermeneutic philosophy. In the former we have him to thank for the original deliberations over the understanding and interpretation of diverse manifestations (articulations) of human spirituality, leading to the evolving of an original though contentious theory of the humanities (*Geisteswissenschaften*). As for hermeneutic philosophy, the ultimate emergence of which we owe to Heidegger and Gadamer, Dilthey undoubtedly holds the credit for positioning the operation of understanding in the context of life, within the philosophy of life that he had spent many years working on. This occurred in the late phase of his work, more widely known from materials published only after his death.

If we take a closer look at the subject-matter tackled by this Berlin scholar in his published papers, the total absence of ethical issues there is astonishing. As such, one cannot be surprised by the fact that two monographs giving an introduction to Dilthey's thinking – one Polish, by Zbigniew Kuderowicz, and the other German, written by Matthias Jung – do not contain a single chapter dedicated *explicite* to a discussion of this philosopher's ethical views.[1] Likewise in regard to two valuable monographs recently published in Poland regarding this scholar, written by Elżbieta Paczkowska-Łagowska,a sage in Polish research into Dilthey, and Leszek Brogowski, representing a younger generation of

[1] Cf. M. Jung, *Dilthey zur Einführung*, Junius Verlag, Hamburg 1996 and Z. Kuderowicz, *Dilthey*, Wiedza Powszechna, Warsaw 1987.

researchers.[2] The lack of discourse on ethical issues is not made up for by the discussion of Dilthey's views regarding such matters as worldview or values. But one cannot make an accusation out of this deficiency, because among the papers published during Dilthey's lifetime there are none in which this brilliant and systematic mind would tackle *explicite* issues of the philosophical understanding of man's moral life. Does this mean that Dilthey was silent about these issues, that he did not even develop the germs of a position of his own?

Such a claim does not reflect the truth. When we take a closer look at Dilthey's intellectual biography, we find not without surprise that he devoted his doctoral dissertation – delivered in 1864 – to ethical issues. Its title in Latin was *De principiis ethicis Schleiermachi*, and it was, one may conclude, dedicated to an analysis and presentation of Schleiermacher's ethics. Dilthey wrote his post-doctoral thesis – entitled *An Attempt at Analysing the Moral Consciousness*[3] – in the same year, but this was not published during his lifetime. Nine years later he writes the first draft of his most important work, i.e. *Einleitung in die Geisteswissenschaften*, in which we find a paper entitled *Über das Studium des Geschichte der Wissenschaft vom Menschen, der Gesellschaft und dem Staat*, in which – as he says himself – he makes an attempt at grasping the "connection of morality with other sciences regarding society and its healthy development."[4]

This means that issues of ethics were important to him from the very start of his academic activities. However, he considered them so complicated, that he only undertook their first reasonably systematic study in 1890, when preparing a university lecture on ethics. This never did acquire a form ready for printing, yet its published form in volume six of the *Gesammelte Schriften* shows that Dilthey held a sufficiently distinct position in matters of morality that it would be worth being tempted to carry out its brief reconstruction. This is because it unveils a way of thinking about morality that is characteristic not only of Dilthey himself, but of the hermeneutic philosophy of life in general. As such, it could become an interesting and important point of reference for elaborating a hermeneutical ethics – understood as an ethics practiced from a hermeneutic point of view.

If one is to believe the drafts and notes stored in the Berlin archives, then Dilthey's lecture opened with the following words:

> In recent years three treatises on ethics have been published at this university. They all represent a utilitarian system. As a certain rule in the assessment of activities, as used by Bentham, this

[2] This refers to the book by Elżbieta Paczkowska-Łagowska, *Logos życia*, słowo/ obraz terytoria, Gdańsk 2000 and L. Brogowski, *Świadomość i historia*, słowo/ obraz terytoria, Gdańsk 2004.

[3] *Versuch einer Analyse des moralischen Bewußtseins*; currently in W. Dilthey, *Gesammelte Schriften*, ed. G. Misch (cited later as GS), vol. VI, Stuttgart – Göttingen 1978, pp. 1-55.

[4] W. Dilthey, *GS*, vol. V, pp. 31 et seq. [transl. from the Polish – J. Weber].

has been widely recognised. I shall show, however, that although within defined borders it can be applied as such a rule, when [treated] as a utilitarian philosophical position it does not conform to contemporary science. If I question it, this is not in order to restore earlier theories, for example those of Kant, Herbart or the English moralists. All that has been shrugged off (*abgetan*). It is rather that we demand that man be represented in his full reality. And in his core, he comes across as a bundle of instincts (*Bündel der Triebe*); and as such an instinct-based unity he creates society. So it is not about refreshing obsolete theories, but about [understanding] how moral processes emerge from this. If I am fighting with the utilitarians in my lecture, this is because their views do not satisfy the demands of contemporary science.[5]

Every serious philosophical position, believes Dithey, must indicate conclusions deriving from its theoretical diagnoses, and principles relating to how human individuals should shape and lead their lives, as well as how society should function. The philosophical discipline dealing with this aspect is philosophical ethics, whose sense of existence this Berlin philosopher does not question. Ethics was hitherto – apart from a few exceptions – the ethics of "concern regarding oneself," of a meaningful and valuable life. However, contemporary ethics cannot – claims Dilthey – remain an individual ethics: it must become social ethics to an equal degree.

In the structure of the psyche, thought (reflection) is – as Cassirer rightly stated – situated between stimulus and reaction: it helps the organism react in the best possible way to stimuli coming from one's surroundings by taking the appropriate action. Cognition (and thought in general) thus intrinsically serves life practice. And this applies not only to colloquial and scientific cognition, but also philosophical reflection, which is not fully achieved in pure, theoretical contemplation, but finds its fulfilment ("its highest goal") in action. "Only full of life-giving forces is practical philosophy truly great" (GS X, p. 13).[6] Its task is to define what has real value and significance in man's life. However, the importance of ethical philosophical reflection depends on the historical era: it waxes at times of "storm and stress," in moments of cultural revolution, the rupturing of cultural continuity, while it wanes in times elapsing in peace, under the unquestioned rule of defined forms of ethicality, when life proceeds along its established trajectory. Dilthey perceives his contemporary epoch,

---

[5] W. Dilthey, "System der Ethik," in idem, *Gesammelte Schriften*, vol. X, Stuttgart – Göttingen 1981, pp. 11-12). The authors of three ethical treatises then published at the University of Berlin were Paulsen, Gizycki and Döring. Commentators also note that when speaking of "the latest research," Dilthey had in mind (inter alia) two books that had then only just been published – A. Horwicz, *Die Analyse der qualitativen Urteile* (Magdeburg 1878) and G.H. Schneider, *Der tierische Wille. Systematische Darstellung und Erklärung der tierischen Triebe und deren Entstehung, Entwicklung und Verbreitung im Tierreich als Grundlage zu einer vergleichenden Willenslehre* (Leipzig 1880) [transl. from the Polish – J. Weber].

[6] So as not to unnecessarily multiply the footnotes, from here on I shall give in brackets the page numbers in the treatise constituting the basis of these analyses (cf. footnote 5) [all these quotations translated from the Polish version – J. Weber].

marked by the Nietzschean slogan "the death of God," as belonging to the former category. In his opinion it is characterised by three main phenomena: (1) a growing dominance of the perception of man as an animal being; (2) the emergence of the "social issue" (elimination of social inequalities, class oppression, the establishing of the ideology of socialism); (3) abandonment of the theory of "double truth" (religious and scientific) regarding the source of what is ideal, leading to the conclusion that there exists "either the ideal born within this world or none."

These facts show that "what is old has already been worn out, while scientific theories have broken the foundations on which was based the importance of the elements of society" (GS X, p. 17). The "eternal validity of Christianity" proved a pipe dream, with attempts at saving it by claiming that "every era must interpret it anew" in order for it to remain alive and significant. And so the burden of drawing up new rules for the ethical functioning of individuals and societies lands on the shoulders of philosophy. But it is unable to satisfactorily resolve it without taking into consideration the results of contemporary social and biological sciences or the humanities. Neither may it omit the reverse conditioning of individual ethicality by social institutions in which the individual fulfils their existence, such as family, ownership, upbringing, social community, state or law.

Dilthey claims that philosophical ethics to date has developed three fundamental methods for coping with the task of "creating rules for life." The first of these, the metaphysical method, "draws everlasting, universally binding principles of evaluating and leading life from the notion of a certain world order (*Weltzusammenhang*)" (GS X, p. 18). Because of the manner in which the said order is portrayed, this method may be manifested in a variety of ways:

(a) as the "metaphysics of the world's moral reason" (deriving from divine bestowment),

(b) as the "metaphysics of contemplative reason" (*beschauliche Vernunft*), based on the negation of earthly reality (articulated in mysticism, gnosis and contemplation),

(c) as the "metaphysics of the creative forces," tied to the principle of self-preservation (ethical reason derives here not from the existence of a personal God, but from the natural creative forces, while the ideal ascendant here is one's own perfection), and

(d) as materialistic metaphysics, deriving from man's animality.

The second of the methods indicated above gives primacy to inner experience: the significance of life and the purposes of action are defined here on the basis of inner experience given in self-awareness. Only here can one discern what is metaphysical, what steps beyond the sphere of material existence. According to this approach the ethical process has sufficient basis and its sole purpose in the person: the individual is a sovereign moral subject, an ethical "purpose in itself" (GS X, p. 21). The ethical rules may be drawn from the self-experience given to a person, and specifically – from the sense of freedom characterising this person, and thus – responsibility for their actions. This feeling does not have to translate to metaphysical statements that cannot be demonstrated, relating to the indeterminacy of reality (existence). This is because the concept of freedom that comes into play here is not metaphysical, it does not proclaim anything regarding the external (physical) or inner (psychic) world. It only names a certain state of awareness, i.e. a feeling, that accompanies certain associations of experience within me.

Such a stance sees the basis for development of moral forms in individual conscience. However, the latter – notes Dilthey – is a certain form of will, a life attitude, and not the content of will. Thus this point of view has a problem coping with relativistic consequences, i.e. the relativity of moral principles, which begin in the essentially subjective inner experience. Their variability is undoubtedly tied to the transformations of culture, the consideration of which causes a certain problem in this approach. Which is why our Berlin humanist reaches the conclusion that "only investigation of the entire organisation of the historical development of ethical life, i.e. taking a social-historical point of view, may truly resolve the issues of ethics" (GS X, p. 22).

The third of the methods, constituting a study of mass-scale moral phenomena, is close to this. Despite its assumption being the existence of individual moral awareness based on awareness of freedom, what is constitutive for this approach is the assumption that the "ethical process does not take place in an isolated individual, but in social and historical coexistence" (GS X, p. 24). This stance results in social ethics, manifested in specific treatises in two fundamental ways (Dilthey speaks of "fractions"): the German fraction, and the French-English fraction. The former derives social evolution, including moral, from the historical process that realises human sagacity, while the latter links it to the realm of biological needs, to the evolution of man as a "political animal."

The dispute of the first three approaches demands epistemic critique, leading to a critical consolidation of ethics. (The fourth, naturalistic, negating the autonomous character of morality, remains an area of his deliberations). None of them, claims Dilthey, "is able to interpret facts [belonging to] the world of morality and derive [from there] generally binding rules" (GS X, p. 26). Yet this does not mean that our Berlin philosopher totally rejects these paths: he only negates their one-sidedness and the resultant simplifications. This is because he is convinced – and this is undoubtedly in keeping with his philosophy of life – that inner experience is the proper starting point for ethical research,[7] that it actually does contain certain components that can be described as metaphysical, and that taking into account research into society and history is essential for a full understanding of ethical phenomena. However, without a studious investigation of what is given in inner experience, we will not achieve – he says – a compromise between the three positions given above. And that is because only this would enable an overcoming of the consequences of evolutionistic positions, for which moral processes must come across as essentially insignificant, as marginal phenomena accompanying the evolution of organisms and species, phenomena unable to influence this evolution and, *ergo*, unable to alter the course of world history.

On the other hand it creates hope for coping with the logical error that the metaphysical stance falls into. The actual principles of conduct (behaviour), including moral principles, are born in the structure of spiritual life (the psyche) from a synthesis of individual understandings, resulting from collisions with reality (i.e. from experience), in the form of a certain volitional disposition. There is no theory that would be purely theoretical in character while at the same time defining life. Metaphysical generalisations are therefore also conditioned by volitional acts, although they seem not to notice this. They are what make it possible to take into account the differentiation already existing in life (and not only in theory) between what is lower and what is higher; what is of less and what is of greater value. An adequate clarification of this distinction may only be carried out on the basis of analysis of inner experience, thanks to "self-contemplation" (*Selbstbesinnung*). Ethics is only possible based on such contemplation, as only this is capable of creating a synthesis of the three above paths leading to a philosophical theory of morality.

However, such a compromise is also offered by utilitarianism, a trend that was very expansive in Dilthey's day. In his opinion, though, it is an illusory compromise. Due to the popularity of this view of ethics, it blocks the path to a critical grounding of ethics through its simplifications. Dilthey therefore feels forced in a way to criticise it. A thorough discussion and contemplation

[7] "In der inneren Erfahrung ist unter allen Umständen der Ausgangspunkt. Allein der Boden der inneren Erfahrung ist fest und sicher. Auf diesem allein kann das metaphysische Bewußtsein sich begründen, und daher ist nur eine kritische Behandlung der Außenwelt imstande, zwischen der innern Erfahrung, dem Bewußtsein von der Gedankenmäßigkeit der Welt und den Erkenntnissen der Naturwissenschaft ein Einverständnis herzustellen," says Dilthey, GS X, p. 27 ("The starting point is always in inner experience. Because only the ground that inner experience constitutes is solid and reliable. It is the only thing one can base metaphysical consciousness on, and that is why only a critical grasp of the external world is capable of generating conformity between awareness of the intellectual character of the world and the diagnoses of the natural sciences.") [transl. from the Polish – J. Weber].

of this matter would split asunder the framework of this chapter; as such, we shall restrict ourselves to but an indication of the fundamental issues.

Utilitarianism is based *explicite* on a connection of the social-historical view (the evolutionary method) with a certain analysis of inner experience. The latter may be seen for example in the reference to feelings such as pleasure, unpleasantness, pain, or a sense of happiness. However, utilitarians are *implicite* forced to refer also to certain metaphysical theses, and this despite their open criticism of idealistic ethics. John Stuart Mill, one of its chief representatives, defines morality as the totality of norms of human behaviour, the fulfilment of which brings a state of happiness into society in the broadest possible scope. Jeremy Bentham in turn, another luminary of this trend, acknowledges the point of view of individual happiness as the starting point for developing theories of moral actions and principles. In his opinion, principles of universal good, i.e. steering will towards what is good, should be at the foundations of all legislative acts, as only this would ensure the greatest happiness for the largest number of people.

Mill – says Dilthey – accepts that the ultimate goal of any human behaviour (the 'highest good' as understood by ancient philosophy) is, for the individual, an existence devoid of pain and abundant in pleasure. This goal also constitutes a criterion of ethicality adopted by utilitarianism. The principle of maximising pleasure and minimising suffering (understood both qualitatively and quantitatively) is emphasised by establishing sanctions for breaking it (physical, social, political and religious sanctions). Their task is to reinforce the motivational force of defined rules, thereby leading to their internalisation. In such a concept – says Dilthey – something such as an inner, autonomous voice of conscience or a guilty conscience does not really have any raison d'être. However, it does lead him to the fundamental question, of whether ethical distinctions that culminate in the conceptual opposition of "right" and "wrong," and which we apply for assessing a variety of actions and inclinations, can be reduced to the opposition of "pleasant – unpleasant" without any semantic loss. And he is just as sceptical in this matter as in regard to the conscience being grasped purely as a reflex of the consciousness regarding external consequences of an action.

Dilthey discerns a strength in utilitarianism in the fact that "it perceives articulations of ethicality as products of advanced psychic development, as complex phenomena" (GS X, p. 33), and not – as in idealistic ethics – as a work (product) of some ethical source of power rooted in human sagacity. The problem lies only – in his opinion – in the fact that utilitarianism does not analyse these phenomena adequately. "What is ethical," says Dilthey, "can only be understood as a product of certain development," while "the beginning of ethical education cannot be other than that rightness is associated with pleasure, and wrongness – with pain [...]" (GS X, p. 37). Being moral or ethical is not something that would reside in the natural inclination of man as a biological species. It is rather a product of the battle with nature, a "victory of a reflective, conscious wanting over instinct. Valour, truth and purity are learned by man" (GS X, p. 38). Utilitarian ethics legitimately emphasises the arduous struggles that led to individuals subjugating their natural instincts to what is socially desirable.

However, by emphasising the educational role of the community in introducing the individual to moral life, by including ethical education and sanctions for violating the rules, and also by emphasising the role of the feeling of sympathy, utilitarianism undermines – in Dilthey's opinion – the individualistic and eudaimonistic assumptions on which it is based. At the point where the principle of individual development, standing up to the mechanisations of society, leads to the propounding of the "obligation of self-fulfilment," utilitarianism is forced to resort to ideas alien to its initial theoretical stance. And this – claims our Berlin philosopher – leads to the "withdrawal from a ystem of individual freedom and replacing it with a system of steering the individual right down to their deepest convictions" (GS X, p. 40). Then, when commenting on the main thread, he adds: "This entire eudaimonism is but a psychic semblance of morality. The real motivations (*Bewegungsgründe*) are totally different. [...] Great historical development could not be achieved only as a result of eudaimonism" (GS X, p. 41).

Dissatisfied with the utilitarian analysis of inner experience, Dilthey sets about his own research, and starts by ascertaining that this experience contains such phenomena as responsibility, commitments, awareness of freedom, self-oblivion or sacrifice. These constitute the "most beautiful flower" of this experience; they did not grow directly from our animality, and neither are they the transformation of instinctive life. Their existence leads to the unresolvable antinomy between the empirical (though subjective) fact of conscience and the hypothetical theory of evolution.

Although inner experience cannot be derived from the theory of evolution, the reverse would – believes Dilthey – rather be possible.[8] "The most general principle of cognition is: this entire world is a phenomenon of my consciousness, it is its fact. From here comes the real grasp of inner states, the phenomenality of all components of the outside world, their practical

[8] Such a stance results from Dilthey's adopted "principle of awareness" or "principle of phenomenality" (*Satz der Phänomenalität*), close to the phenomenological demonstrating of the essence of phenomena in the record of a given pure consciousness. For a broader discussion compare M. Jung, *Dilthey...*, op. cit.

usefulness as a system of signs relating to what is independent of us" (GS X, p. 45). In the semantic difference given in these signs, various ways of existing for these phenomena are "co-given"; their grasping is only rendered possible by the adequate situating of ethical phenomena. Any reductionism makes this impossible. "At every moment," says Dilthey, "I experience how from a feeling emerges an instinctual aspiration to withhold it. I experience how the aftermath of pain is turning one's back [on its source], and then hatred towards it. Yet I cannot step beyond this vitality of my own. The being-given of a feeling, of presentation, of wanting, cannot be boiled down to an impression and a sensation. If I do that, then I am doing away with inner experience, in keeping with which the presentation, wanting, feeling always remain something distinguished, and I put in their place something occurring in the thought process, which after all only emerges through the mediation of differentiation and interaction (*Sonderung und Zusammenwirkung*)" (GS X, p. 46).

"*Der Mensch ist ein Bündel von Triebe*" (man is a bundle of instincts) – this statement sets out the direction of the Diltheyesque founding of ethics. This is a direction in which what is psychic is connected to what is biological, because the former makes up the internal structure of the latter, and the latter – of the former. As for the entirety, it harmonises with the idea of evolution at least in the sense that a comparison of the lives of lower and higher organised animals and man downright demands its introduction: as a way of explaining more complex forms of psyche on the basis of – or also by relating to – more basic forms.

Aestheticizing or intellectualistic depictions of man's nature falsify its true image, overlooking the fundamental fact that this "bundle of instincts" that is man is held in check thanks to force of will. "You can only understand history," says Dilthey, "when you understand the central role of great volitional processes" (GS X, p. 50). This is why these particular processes will constitute the centre of his own consolidation of ethics. The starting point is therefore the nature of the psyche, and in particular – of the volitional processes taking place in man.

The basic schema of life is, in Dilthey's opinion, relatively simple. Response to a stimulus is meant to restore the equilibrium between organism and surroundings. Animals are equipped with the instinctual mechanism of reflex, which enables their deliberate influence on the external world in order to adjust to it. As the level of complexity of organisms increases, there is a separating of individual organs that produce the appropriate psychic processes. Reoccurring stimuli produce mechanisms of re-identification, followed by the mechanism of accustomization, which activates the memory and perceptual representations. The process of differentiation and growth in the level of complication of organs and functions follows. The simple initial system of "stimulus – reaction" becomes complicated. Urges occur as accompanying animal functions, generating an entire instinctual system. "Psychic creations, sensations, perceptions, representations, thoughts, feelings, moods, affections, urges and wants differ from each other, while the reverse action by such an organism, with the goal of adjusting to the outside world, splits into manifold movements, largely steered by the mechanism of reflex" (GS X, p. 49).

The connection of instinct with the feeling that accompanies it is a trick of nature, it is the equipment of organisms possessing psyche, enabling their non-intellectual cognition of reality and usage of its resources for survival and growth. Thanks to the regular connection of the relationship of usefulness of some element of one's environment with a feeling of pleasure accompanying its acquisition, instincts that enable survival, reproduction and proliferation are reinforced. "When now, via the connection of sensations in perceiving and thinking, the grasp of the outside world in a more fundamental manner, through the connection of feelings and instincts, raises value-giving assessment above what is momentary and self-interested, then the match between individual and their environment [...] becomes increasingly perfect, as a result of which their psychic purpose increases. Even in the highest creations of historical life such is the fundamental structure of what is animate. All puzzles of historical accomplishments and the history of existence may be solved only on the basis of this biological plan of existence (*Daseins*)" (GS X, pp. 49-50).

By treading further along this road, Dilthey distinguishes diverse classes of instincts and the chains that they create. In reference to the statement that hunger, love or war constitute mighty forces of the moral world, Dilthey isolates the instinct of feeding, the instinct of reproduction (and the care of offspring that accompanies this)and the instincts of protection and defence. In his occasionally meticulous analyses, he strives to show how these instincts transform into affections and passions. To this he adds the instinct of movement, and the instinct of reassurance. The fact that the mechanism for executing these instincts may, in man, be halted by the force of his will (which cannot be achieved, for example, in the case of breathing), gives him the ability to distinguish constraining ethics (e.g. Kant) and ethics negating corporeality, the instinctual sphere (e.g. Arthur Schopenhauer), which he confronts with ethics shaping urges. He sees a representative of the latter in Schleiermacher. He would probably also agree for Max Scheler to be added to this group.

Dilthey sees the first displays of ethical phenomena in vitality manifesting itself as a feeling of one's own power, later courage, that draws from awareness of one's own strength, sometimes passing into boldness or temerity, to then achieve fulfilment in perseverance at work, in the planning of actions, in subjecting one's will to the goals one has set. The volitional act here proceeds in three stages: a system of needs forms on the instincts and their accompanying feelings; these needs in turn evoke the imposing of will, leading to the harmonising of man's relations with his surroundings; diverse forms of fulfilment and satisfaction then flow from these actions. "This is what is involved in the surrendering of your will to [the service of] grand life goals surpassing the individual, systems of culture, and diverse bonds" (GS X, p. 64).

A certain moulding of will (*Willensbeschaffenheit*), which perceptions of the results of our deeds have some influence on, is decisive for the emergence of ethicality. This moulding of will is also subject to a judgment of valuation. An ethical judgment may be phrased as the reflection of the value that this moulding of will holds for us. It is thanks to this that sympathy, mercy, compassion, kindness and respect are assessed positively. One should not conclude, just because the execution of ethical deeds evokes a feeling of happiness or satisfaction, that they are carried out "for" these feelings. They only accompany them, reinforcing the shaping of the will that "produced" them. Dilthey rejects the "morality of wellbeing" (*Wohlfahrtmoralität*), i.e. the concept that sees the sources of our ethicality in the search for prosperity, euphoria or good fortune.

Our Berlin philosopher discerns an important factor in the development of morality in upbringing. It is thanks to this process that we learn to mimic others, and thereby – to understand them, their worthy reasons, motives, and ideals.[9] We are confronted with something that goes beyond our self-interest, with a certain ideality. This happens first in the family, then at school, after which it is literature that furthers ethical education.[10]

Dilthey analyses a number of other attitudes (lasting mouldings of will) that are of significance to the phenomenon of morality, such as bond, commitment, openness to strangers, treating others like people, and truthfulness.

[9] This is in keeping with the first version of Dilthey's hermeneutics, according to which to understand a work or deed means to inquire through experience into the original act of its creation, to recreate it in the mind, as if imitating its author. When talking of the first version what we have in mind is *Einleitung in die Geisteswissenschaften* (1883) and smaller treatises related to this work. We know the second and more mature version of his hermeneutics from writings publishes partially posthumously (mainly *Aufbau der geschichtlichen Welt in den Geisteswissenschaften,* 1910 and later additions. I give a broader presentation of the development of Dilthey's hermeneutic theory in my book *Hermeneutyczny zwrot...*, op. cit.

[10] In a postscript Dilthey writes that the natural sciences do not prepare a person for functioning in society in a manner based on sympathy and kindness. Research into nature is conducive to shaping a clear mind, but the development of the highest ethical attributes is connected to contact with the most brilliant figures of history and literature (GS X, p. 84). As we can see, Dilthey does not mention here for example philosophical treatises focusing on ethics, granting high and historical literature primacy in shaping the ethical attitudes of human individuals. He thereby anticipates the theses of Ricoeur and Rorty.

As a philosopher of life, he is convinced of the interweaving of diverse forces and tendencies in spiritual life, which makes it impossible to precisely give and put order to these germs of morality. Within the essence of each one of them is the desire for repetition of certain volitional mind-sets or the reinforcing of certain personality properties. But where – one could ask – lies the criterion that would allow us to qualify them as proto-ethical? Dilthey writes little on this matter. At one point, contemplating the ethicality of courage, he states: "we can define courage as an ethical germ because it is connected to raising the sense of life to a higher level" (GS X, p. 84). And that in turn gives rise to a tendency to assess it positively.

However, one must not forget – adds Dilthey – that "natural circulation" exists, as a result of which not only do actions lead to feelings, but also feelings lead to actions. Neither may one make light of the significance of accustomization, as a proto-moral force, or of the role of form of behaviour, which – as based on a certain rule – is situated above the relationship between desire and satisfaction.

Dilthey devotes the final section of his lecture, entitled *Evolution of what is moral, and the principles of social ethics*, to the transformations that the germs of ethicality developed in man are undergoing, and the relation between these germs and the "ethical complexes of force" functioning within society. Volitional acts – he says – connected to a feeling of some kind of commitment, and the joy from fulfilling it, have little in common with the relationship of sensual desire – sensual pleasure. The satisfying of urges – and Schopenhauer knew this perfectly – is always momentary, temporary, while states linked to the germs of ethicality provide lasting satisfaction. This is why society attaches such importance to their existence and their development. They are what guarantees its stability and increase in prosperity. As a consequence, the evolution of moral life, constituting a result of social evolution, has a reverse influence. One could say that what is social interweaves dialectically with what is ethical. Because of their connection, it is impossible to give an a priori answer to the question of what is moral and what is not, or to discern the evolution of morality from a few arbitrarily selected examples. "Only what that evolution does with the ethical forces is ethical or good" (GS X, p. 87).

It would seem that what is decisive here is that moment of relative durability. This is what allows Dilthey to distinguish between lower and higher properties of will, and to posit the theorem that if there is concentration only on the former, this will lead to conflict with the latter. This is because at an animal level – though in regard to this area the highest such – a fundamental question that arises is: What is the point of all that life? Only strong and positive emotions drawing from contribution to the existence of lasting satisfaction, meaning satisfaction with life in a society functioning collectively, are capable of giving an individual an existentially satisfying answer to this question. The grand principle of active life, claims the Berlin philosopher, is joy from every exertion of will that is connected to the solidarity of interests within society. However, the pra-phenomenon is neither the kind of ethicality flowing from the divine and purely spiritual nature of man, nor the kind deriving from the optimal organisation of society, but is the kind that is born thanks to individual moral germs that emerged as a result of biological and social evolution.

This evolution does not follow the rational laws of history, of which the individual would be but a blind executor, but occurs as the mutual influence of individual forces within a certain environment. Deriving ethicality from the objective spirit (as defined by Hegel) was alien to Dilthey; he sought it rather within the subjective spirit. Ethical forms of social life are coordinators of reoccurring realisations of those individual forces that, as a result, transform into "social forces of a second order" (p. 88). They cannot be derived solely from usefulness, as utilitarianism would like, as living germs of morality that have come into being in individual deeds constitute the beginning. We owe to them the existence of such phenomena as work, individual development, ownership, communitiness and familiness, etc. Regarding the latter, Dilthey says: "Marriage and family are developing forms of work community that we perceive as insurmountable. Marriage is the realised ideal of the total abolition of alien-ness. It could only materialise on the basis of sexual intercommunity and shared children. Such is the world's greatest secret" (GS X, p. 90). The fact that this thought isonly ostensibly passé can be seen, for example, in Ferdinand Fellmann's book *The Couple. An Erotic Justification of Man.*[11]

Progress in civilisation is leading to a reduction in the forces directed towards the satisfaction of fundamental needs. At first this applies to the more affluent social groups, who focus their attention on issues going beyond the material requirements of the moment. These are the motor of slow moral evolution, since – claims Dilthey, on the basis of Charles Jean Marie Letourneau's work entitled *L'évolution de la morale* of 1884 – there are no general, innate moral rules existing on the lowest steps of civilisation. We owe ethicality to the fundamental right of will, which says that the frequent repetition of similar volitional acts leads to the emergence of habits, which in turn lead to the embedding of a custom, applying to the individual as well as the community (group). "When what is similar (*gleichförmig*) is grasped by the consciousness, a rule of action arises" (p. 91). Its emergence is favourable for the organism, as it removes the

[11] Cf. F. Fellmann, *Para. Erotyczne źródła człowieczeństwa*, transl. J. Duraj, W. Małecki, Wydawnictwo Naukowe UAM, Poznan 2009.

burden from the will. The "automation" of the satisfying of instincts enables the development of needs of a higher order, spiritual needs, with the need for individual self-fulfilment at the forefront. This in turn takes place through the creation of diverse social bonds (love, concern, culture). But this evolution is not capable of quenching urges, which also evolve. Needs emerge for increased consumption, for luxury, for dominance and ruling, needs that suppress the development of ethical awareness. These adverse phenomena are occasionally so powerful, that they even lead to historical catastrophes.

However, Dilthey is aware that at the beginning, i.e. at the birth of historical humanity, what is moral is hard to distinguish from what is in keeping with law or custom. An important role is also played by religion, in which among early peoples there was an interweaving of "science, poetry and faith" (GS X, p. 95). The idealisation of the dead, about whom "you are [were] not allowed to speak ill," evolving into an ancestral cult, is also an important element of moral evolution, as it leads to the emergence and storing in collective memory of personal role models recommended for emulation. And the skill and desire to emulate constitutes – as we have already emphasised on many an occasion – a significant trait in simple mentalities. And thus such a habit becomes a custom, and this in turn joins the moral rules governing this particular community. Ethical ideals become major forces of the social world.

The meaning of the main ethical predicates, good – bad, is undergoing similar evolution. Initially, claims Dilthey, they were used in regard to man capable of performing a particular type of deed. Somebody was good for felling trees, somebody else – good for hunting, and somebody else still – for preparing meals. Only in time did this predicate begin to be linked to being good for performing all human tasks, and thus to something that, till this day, is referred to as moral strengths (ethical virtues). And those of them serving an improvement in the standard of social living, e.g. truthfulness, connected to the need for trust, gradually took shape and strengthened their significance.

"There are means of acting," says Dilthey, "and [personal] traits that are conducive to the formation of society; they ensure fulfilment for individuals, are conducive to people's command of nature, as well as unity and harmony, and close relationships between individuals within the social whole. We define such traits and means of acting as virtues, as what is good, what is ethical. What is defined as conscience, we may try out in relation to these tasks of human life. This is powerful proof of the connection existing between the conscience and the factual tasks of human life" (GS X, pp. 99-100).

Yet despite his historicism, Dilthey is also unable to withhold, if not from giving some kind of timeless principle of ethicality, then at least "drive factors, motors of ethical life." While doing so he rejects the reductionist intentions of boiling them down to something more fundamental, emphasising the pluralism of the forces and motives. In this context he speaks of the need for recognition from others, of sympathy towards others, of kindness and love,[12] of awareness of commitment, of the feeling of duty, and also of legal awareness.[13] Dilthey perceives in the latter the "proper core (*Mark*) of the social shaping of life." He claims that "You can become a decent (*tüchtig*) person without love, but not without integrity (*Rechlichkeit*)" (GS X, p. 103). To these driving forces of personal ethicality, Dilthey adds respect to the autonomous values of what was created in the historical process. He himself describes this as cultural systems, although I believe he would agree to Gadamer's terms of *Überlieferung* (cultural transmission) and tradition (*Tradition*). In his opinion the desire to be involved in this process, if only due to the joy flowing from the imitation of great ideals, the feeling of an influx of vital forces during the overcoming of one's own sloth and laziness, is an important factor conducive to the development of ethical awareness.

This last thought inclines Dilthey to voice a few remarks regarding the relationship occurring between the vital source of ethicality and the ethos of various peoples and ages. Due to the fragmentary and selective character of these reflections we may pass them over here. One thing is clear, though. His deliberations on ethics derive from the philosophy of life that he professed the whole time and that he developed creatively. This is why he is sceptical regarding idealistic ethics, which beneath slogans of the type "uniform moral law" or "voice of conscience" strive to embrace the entirety of moral phenomena within some coherent, closed system. In such ethics – examples of which in his opinion are the ethics of Kant, Fichte and Schleiermacher – "the simplest precepts of conscience and highest subtleties of moral culture act against our will with the same pretension" (GS X, p. 107), the pretension for absolute subjugation. Such an approach to morality must cause a hiatus between moral reality and ethical theory. "The contradictions of ethics to date," he writes, "establishing unconditional ethical judgments, can only be removed when taking a close look at the very concept of unconditional ethical judgment, or better – of duty, commitment [...]. Such a simple duty, everywhere equal, from which would derive a system of commitments accompanying it

[12] Anticipating Fellmann (and passing Heidegger in this point) Dilthey says: "Only in love is there a broadening of being-here-as (*des Daseins*) beyond the sphere of the self itself (*Selbst*), and through that – the removal of egotism" (p. 102). Cf. F. Fellmann, *Para...*, op. cit.

[13] And then in turn anticipating Ricoeur (*Oneself as Another*, transl. K. Blamey, Chicago and London, 1992) Dilthey states that loyalty to oneself, linked to the sense of one's own identity, leads to the will for abiding by commitments towards others, treated as persons the same as myself (p. 102).

and everywhere equal, simply does not exist" (p. 108). After all, our commitments are of very varied types.

Such an observation forces Dilthey to recognise the pluralism of ethical concepts, conditioned by the difference in the form of commitment, which is the basis of each of them. Analysis inclines him to put forward three basic forms of duty. They are:

(1) commitments that have emerged based on the relationship of recognition (*Anerkennung*) – of others and by others – within a certain human alliance (nation, state, party, etc.). Legal relations are an example, although this type of commitment is not exhausted in them. It generates an attitude of integrity, of honesty (*Rechtschaffenheit*). This is related to our participation in the structure of public life, in the social division of work, and to our place in society. Refusal to acknowledge commitments of this kind discards one beyond the confines of a certain social relationship;

(2) goodwill or kindness towards others constitutes a different form of duty. There is no feeling of coercion here, as present in (1), one's will is freer, while the attitude towards others is more personal and individual. Submitting to this form of duty takes on a variety of forms. Its rejection leads to exclusion from the "sphere of mutual sacrifice and devotion" (GS X, p. 112);

(3) duty of yet another form is that towards the ideals that motivate one's life, steered by the aspiration for it to have a certain autonomous value, for it to be fulfilled, complete, and in a way perfect (*vollkommen*). Negating this duty (this ideal) excludes one from "idealistic existences belonging to the spirit of the world" (GS X, p. 112).

The fulfilment of each of these duties may be accompanied by a feeling of joy, of fulfilment, of pleasure, although this is not their cause. The main motive here is the desire for a 'worthy, good life', in which our will relates to the sphere of ideals and values lending our finite existence an existential depth. These motivations – adds Dilthey – cannot be derived in full purely from analyses of the structure of inner experience ("the nature of the human soul," GS X, p. 112); because one has to take into account the nature of the environment in which it is realised: the nature of the society, the state, the money, etc. These last components, as filling morality with concrete, historical content, complete the purely formal factors developed during the analysis of our inner experience. One has but to realise how diversely these same ideals (i.e. the ideal of bravery or abstinence) are actually realised in different eras or cultures.

Chapter 3

Is Fundamental Ontology a Fundamental Ethics?

The titular question is of course connected to the philosophical concept developed by Martin Heidegger (1889-1976), which as we know was against what was – in his opinion – the unilaterally and epistemologically directed phenomenological philosophy of Edmund Husserl and the similarly oriented neo-Kantianism of both the Baden and Marburg Schools, and so the three directions then dominating in Germany, acknowledging the theory of cognition as *prima philosophia*. Heidegger, who considered such an approach short-sighted, put forward the idea of the rehabilitation of ontology as a first philosophy, i.e. as the basis of philosophy, placing in his main work, *Being and Time*, published in 1927, the thesis that the fundamental philosophical question is not that about cognition, about its methods or criteria, but a question about being, or to put it differently: about the sense of being, while the path for seeking an answer to this question is analysis, or – as Heidegger put it himself – the analytics of being of such an existence that poses this question at all and is capable of raising it, i.e. human existence. Heidegger, as we know, calls this existence alertness of mind, being-there, existence (*das Dasein* in German), while the theory that is the explication of this analytics of the human being he calls fundamental ontology, i.e. the foundation of ontology.[1]

[1] Neither of the translations of the term *Dasein* (as*being*, proposed by Bogdan Baran, or as *consciousness* proposed by Krzysztof Michalski), though they have certain strengths, are free of significant faults. As such some Polish experts on Heidegger (e.g. Paweł Dybel) prefer to use the original term. In Wojciech Herman's book *Próba ugruntowania metafizyki* (Oficyna Wydawnicza Politechniki Warszawskiej, Warsaw 2008) a new translation of this term was recently proposed, original and at the same time relatively adequate in relation to Heidegger's

After the publication of *Being and Time*, and following the enormous success this work enjoyed, Heidegger was questioned by students, listeners and readers – as expressed in a few of his papers, including his *Letter on humanism* – asking "when are you going to write an ethics?", i.e. supplement fundamental ontology with practical philosophy, a main part of which normally comprises the theory of morality. Heidegger usually shrugged his shoulders in answer to this question, a gesture that could be interpreted in at least two ways. The first is that there is no point in writing or working on a philosophical ethics. Philosophical ethics is a groundless undertaking, one without perspective, defective, corrupted by the error of subjectivism resulting from the adoption of a certain ideal of being a person (a human being), which others by no mean have to share. And ethics based on such an ideal, not universally shared, would not be binding. The second interpretation of this shrugging of the shoulders that appears here would sound more or less as follows: "there is no need to write anything more at all, because fundamental ontology is also the fundamental ethics."[2] Why should I – Heidegger seems to be saying – work on additional ethics constituting the completion of my fundamental ontology, since in the work *Being and Time* this ethics is immanently contained? In order to answer this question, so as to check whether this really is the case, it would be worth adding to the question about ethics contained in *Being and Time* another question: how fairs the matter with ethics following the so-called "turn"?

This is because Heidegger soon proved to be not fully satisfied with the shape his main work had taken on. He felt that it had been written from what was still a transcendental position, from the perspective of the philosophy of subjectiveness, adjusted only to take into account the historicity, factuality, and situationality of human existence. *Das Dasein* (consciousness/being/spending time), which in fundamental ontology enters a distinguished place occupied until now by transcendental awareness, actually signifies a certain important change of approach, but it does conserve a certain domination of human existence, of a human perspective. This is particularly explicit in the grasp of understanding from the point of view of an immanent "temporalisation" of human existence. The most important dimension of this temporalisation is the future, and therefore human intention and human will, which Heidegger strongly accentuates, tying understanding with the projecting of the being of an understood existence. I understand a pen as a pen if I am capable of using it as "something serving to write," i.e. if I can project inside my head precisely

intentions, as »sojourn« or »spending time, dwelling«. According to the author, the idea for this translation came from prof. Ulrich Schrade.

[2] This roadis taken by Krzysztof Stachewicz in his book *Problem ugruntowania moralności. Studium z etyki fundamentalnej*, Wydawnictwo Naukowe Semper, Warsaw 2006.

such a deed carried out with its help. Therefore it is my subjectiveness that settles the sense of existences that I encounter. Because of this in the 30s of the twentieth century a change is made to his approach to practising philosophy, defined as a "turn" (*Kehre*). This turn is manifested in the strongest manner in his work entitled *Beiträge zur Philosophie (Vom Ereignis),* published quite late – in the sixties – despite having been written earlier.[3]

This of course gives rise to the question about whether the ethical thread is also present in his late philosophy, which could also be described as ontology, though no longer fundamental. Because although human existence no longer plays the role of foundation here, it is – at least until a certain moment – a type of ontology, because the question about existence, about the sense of being in general, remains the supreme question of this philosophy. Although it is not easy to define whether the inclusion of the ethical issue in his late philosophy can be determined, it is worth being tempted to supplement the question about ethics in *Being and Time* with reflection regarding the place of ethics in Heidegger's late thinking, e.g. via analysis of a paper written after the war, in the spirit of the transformations taking place in his philosophy, and namely his *Letter on humanism.*[4] This broadening of the material base is justified if only for the reason that explicit comments regarding ethics are to be found there.

Presuming the reader has a certain basic knowledge of *Being and Time*, one of the canons of 20th-century philosophy, let us point only – very superficially – to those elements of this work that may be linked to ethics.

Heidegger makes no secret of desiring to restore ontology; after all, be believes – despite warnings from the likes of Husserl, Heinrich Rickert, Hermann Cohen and Paul Natorp –that not existence but the being of an existence is a phenomenon not in the colloquial sense, but in a truly phenomenological sense.[5] The entire history of philosophy, he says, can be reconstructed as focused around the interpretation of being that is dominant in a given era or philosophical concept, around the understanding of what it means "to be." But, he adds, these interpretations are most often camouflaged and one has to have pretty good phenomenological-hermeneutic skills to detect them. This is

[3] M. Heidegger, *Contributions to Philosophy*, trans. P. Emad and K. Maly, Indiana University Press, Indiana 1999.

[4] The germs of difficult though naturally legitimate searches for ethical issues in Heidegger's late philosophy are contained in papers by Werner Kogge (including "Technologie des 21. Jahrhunderts. Perspektiven der Technikphilosophie," *Deutsche Zeitschrift für Philosophie* 6/2008) and Hubert Dreyfus (e.g. *Between Techne and Technology: The Ambiguous Place of Equipment in Being and Time*, Tulane Studies in Philosophy 1984, vol. 332).

[5] Cf. M. Heidegger, *Being and Time*, transl. J. Stambaugh, State University of New York Press, New York 1996.

why Heidegger wants *explicite* to pose the question on being and on the reasons for its limbo, for its concealment behind existence, behind what is.

The road to discovering the sense of being in general leads via disclosure of the essence and structure of the being of existence distinguished by the fact that it is capable of posing such a question and – as not only the history of philosophy proves, but so too does the history of art or religion – really does pose it. Quite naturally it is man who is this existence, portrayed by Heidegger not in the perspective of a psychophysical unity or some other definition of man, already ready and adopted by him (e.g. *animal rationale, homo faber, homo ludens*, etc.), but as a being-in-the-world, i.e. as a "place in which existence is revealed." This man, conceived as *Dasein* (a specific existence), is what enables self-presentation of an existence in all of its magnificence.

The sense of non-human existence is determined by human ability to understand (perceive) being, which in turn defines the temporal character of human existence. What the temporalisation of *Dasein* involves is that existence is (1) factual, i.e. thrown into a certain here and now that it does not choose, (2) oriented for surviving in surroundings that it must become familiar with, immersing (falling) into it by influencing it, which in turn is achieved through (3) understanding as projecting the sense of being of understood existences (encountered and created).

Each of these aspects is linked to a different dimension of the time lived through (temporalisation/*eitigung*): throwing with the past, falling with the present, understanding/projecting with the future, the most important – in Heidegger's eyes – dimension of temporalisation.[6] Projecting makes it possible for us to understand existences in new ways, and therefore opens up before us new ways of self-fulfilment, and new ways of self-presentation before that encountered existence.

Conscious existence (*Dasein*), as an existence thrown among other existences, is something ontic, just as they are. As one posing the question about the being of existence, it also becomes an existence, something ontological, as it can create (and it really does create) ontology – knowledge regarding what exists and how.Which is also why philosophical categories serving to describe what is ontic lose their adequacy towards it. Heidegger therefore puts forward the idea of existentials as concepts appropriate for grasping manners of exist-

[6] There is no need to add that this is Heidegger's version of Husserl's conception of the internal awareness of time (expressed using notions such as retention and protention); that Husserl considered retention (the past) the main dimension of time experienced, while Heidegger – projection (the future), says quite a lot about the transfer of emphasis from the contemplative phenomenology of cognising awareness to the activistic philosophy of existence (of life).

ence and the existential structure of a conscious existence. In his *Being and Time* we find a fair number of them, and they include – along side temporalisation – location, attunement, understanding and discourse – to mention but those of greatest importance. Their culmination, constituting a type of connection of various dimensions of existence, is the existential of care unveiling the ontological structure common to every *Dasein*, although manifesting itself in a variety of ontic ways.

Heidegger strives in his analyses to emerge from existence in its everydayness, from the average *Dasein*, so as even in its barely reflected being seek glimmers of existence transgressing the pure ontic. This is why an important aspect of his research is the distinction into proper (translated by many as 'authentic') and improper existence (inauthentic). The difference between them is subtle, as the individual existence of every one of us pulsates between an absolute losing of oneself in unreflective carrying out of what is "being done," in the thinking of what is "being thought," and an authentically experienced existence – flowing from inside – of reflection regarding our participation in the perception and creation of sense, and that not only of our own action, but also of those beings we are relating to in this action.

We are roused to authentic existence by the rarely voiced phenomenon of fear (*Angst*), constituting a type of attunement different to ordinary fright (of something; *Furcht*), ensuing – as Heidegger discloses towards the end of *Being and Time* – from the worry of non-being, i.e. the fear of death. After all the being of a person is a "being-toward-death" (*Sein-zum-Tode*). It is this mood that inclines us to abandon the anonymous existing in how life is lived on average by "the they," that wakes us from that "ontic nap" so we would begin to live ontologically, i.e. fulfilling not the "they," but the self.

This segment of his fundamental ontological reasoning is where Heidegger situates the deliberations on topics usually linked to ethics, which could suggest that this is an ethical section of *Sein und Zeit*. These phenomena are care of oneself, taking care of others (in the modes of properties and non-properties), the dictatorship of anonymous public opinion (of that "the they" – *das Man)*and the necessity of breaking free of its power. In so doing he strongly emphasises the axiological neutrality of his analyses (their purely ontological character), which – in keeping with the phenomenological motto – should remain at the level of description, not moving on either to the level of formulating behavioural norms or the plane of existential appeals. Such a descriptive attitude also applies to the phenomena of guilt and conscience that he discusses.

Claiming that the other is absent in *Sein und Zeit* would be going too far, yet one must agree with the assertion that within this work he is presented mainly in the form of "anonymous others."[7] In the depiction of the other as an *alter ego*, as a person or "face," Heidegger would see too far-reaching philosophical constructs that cannot be rediscovered on the ontological level that he analyses. Even there where a reaction we would define as personal seems to shine through in his arguments, e.g. in his exposure of various ways of caring for others, one can clearly see that he means self-fulfilment, the realising of oneself, and not a self-forgetting ethical opening up to the suffering of another person as one's kin. Which is why in *Sein und Zeit* one has to search for ethical theory almost against the intentions of Heidegger himself, against his direct remarks. However, for many researchers and devotees of his philosophy the temptation is too great to resist.

Let us begin therefore by taking a closer look at selected possible answers to the question about whether fundamental ontology is an ethics, or – putting it even more strongly – fundamental ethics? Let us recall first of all that there are at least two answers in Polish philosophical literature from which the deliberations should begin. And these are two different standpoints. The author of one is Paweł Dybel, and of the other – Krzysztof Stachewicz referred to above, who devoted a 250-page treatise to the issue. Paweł Dybel wrote an article for the collective work *Heidegger dzisiaj* [Heidegger today], published in 1991 by Aletheia, under the title literally meaning *Mr Heidegger, when will you write an ethics?*, in which he referred explicitly to the issue of ethics, as the only such paper in this volume. In his own answer to his titular question, Dybel decidedly rejects the suggestion that fundamental ethics is contained within fundamental ontology.[8]

In his opinion, fundamental ontology – even if Heidegger believes otherwise – cannot be the foundation of ethics, mainly because the ethical phenomena appearing there are portrayed by the author of *Being and Time* too strongly from the point of view of the ontological schemas ruling this work, which leads to a falsification of the phenomenal sense of moral phenomena in general, and in particular of the phenomena acknowledged as ethical that he analyses. What Dybel has in mind is the phenomenon of conscience and the phenomenon of guilt. These are issues that appear in Part One, Division Two of *Being and Time*, entitled *Da-sein and Temporality*. Chapters 55 and 56 touch on

[7] The absence of a phenomenologically appropriate grasp of other human existences in Heidegger's existential structures of *Dasein* was castigated by his first post-doctoral student, Karl Löwith, in *Das Individuum in der Rolle des Mitmenschen*, written under the former's guidance.

[8] Cf. P. Dybel, "Panie Heidegger, kiedy pan napisze etykę," in P. Marciszuk, C. Wodziński (eds), *Heidegger dzisiaj*, Warsaw 1990. Recently another publication appeared tackling Heidegger's attitude towards ethics, the work of R. Strzelecki: *Ethos i wolność. W poszukiwaniu etycznej wymowy* Bycia i czasu *Martina Heideggera*, Wydawnictwo Uniwersytetu Jagiellońskiego, Cracow 2006.

such issues as the existential and ontological foundations of conscience, the character of one's conscience as a call, and the understanding of summons and guilt, etc.

What is Dybel's reasoning? This Warsaw philosopher believes that Heidegger wants to squeeze phenomena into a kind of schema, in a kind of opposition of what is ontic and what is ontological. What is ontic is what is concrete in life, while what is ontological is what is structural, what applies to human existence in its essence. With Heidegger this is linked to a distinction into authentic being and inauthentic being, or in other words into a right being and a wrong being. This inauthentic being is a being taking place only at an ontic level (and is therefore unreflective). Heidegger attempts to describe the phenomena of conscience and guilt as they function in life. In the case of guilt he starts from guilt in the sense of a debt, in the financial sense, of arrears of some kind that one has towards somebody. He adds two other meanings for this word to this, so as to reach the conclusion that guilt thus understood is of an accounting character, it has the character of thinking in terms of settling accounts with somebody. Moving on to an ontological, existential level (i.e. leaving the existentiell, concrete level in life), Heidegger shows that the phenomenon of guilt portrayed properly is, above all, being at fault in relation to oneself, while the theme of settling accounts with somebody is an inauthentic theme. He refers to the phenomenon of conscience in a similar vein. In his authentic, i.e. ontological version, it is also about an answer by hearing the call of conscience, which – as it happens – comes from *Da-sein* itself. The being existing authentically calls itself. Thus this is not the internalised voice of the ethical or moral community in which it lives. Interpretation of the voice of conscience as that originating from outside is what he recognises as inauthentic.

Because of the above, while conceptualising this germ of the ethical phenomenon – meaning of these two elements, the conscience and guilt in which ethicality is as if a self-reference – a certain reduction emerges. There is no room here for the other, for another, for a community, because – in Heidegger's opinion – such ethicality would be something external in relation to *Da-sein*, questioning its freedom of self-determination. Dybel disagrees with this, believing that the Other is unavoidable, i.e. the relation to the other must be taken into account if an ethical phenomenon is to be properly constituted. He adds something that he does not fully clarify, but which as an idea is most certainly valuable, something that he defines as "ethical substantiality."

"In this essay," says Dybel, "taking the way in which Heidegger conducts an existential analysis of the phenomena of conscience and guilt in his *Being and Time* as my starting point, I have tried to show that he does not take into account the specifically ethical sense that has come to be linked to him.

And this to an equal degree in ontic and ontological analysis. The genesis of this phenomenon lies in the fact that the author of *Being and Time* arbitrarily acknowledged the structure of the existence of *Dasein* that he constructed beforehand, comprising two mutually implicating (as in opposition) 'ways of being' of *Da-sein*, as the fundamental and practically the only perspective for considering the phenomena. These are being in a "fallen" way, within which the main objects of care of *Dasein* are objects and issues of the everyday, and being in an authentic way, in which by turning towards itself it unveils before itself that which constitutes the ontological condition of the possibility of its existence. In the meantime the essence of the phenomena of conscience and guilt taken in a strictly ethical sense cannot be grasped within the framework of a structure of this kind, they comprise elements that the existential analysis performed by Heidegger in *Time and Being* is by assumption incapable of taking into account. These elements are – firstly – a defined ethical substantiality, in which both phenomena are rooted, enabling the "I" to adjudicate about something as "good" or "bad" with an apodictic obviousness. Secondly, the experience – at a colloquial level now – of conscience and guilt as something most definitely "one's own," non-replaceable and incomparable with any other inner-worldly measure. Thirdly, the distinct reference to the other as the one towards whom one is at fault in the entire individual uniqueness of their existence."[9]

That would be all as far as Dybel's position – which is probably pretty clear – is concerned. Now for a few comments regarding Stachewicz's position, in opposition to Dybel's, particularly as on one of the pages of his book he says that Dybel's assertions are a misunderstanding.[10] Stachewicz is evidently apt to accept the explanations of Heidegger himself, and recognise that fundamental ontology is the foundation of ethics, that it is fundamental ethics. Admittedly, it is not a normative ethics, and neither can it be transformed into any normative ethics, but – he believes – one can interpret from it a certain type of "par-ethics," which is a contemplation of a certain ontological structure within which it is at all possible for ethicality to emerge.[11] And this is ethicality in the sense of the ethics of authenticity, because Stachewicz is of the opinion that the germs or elements of ethics in *Being and Time* can be boiled down to precisely such an ethics of authenticity. He uses a dichotomy himself here: the metaphysics of morality – the phenomenology of morality. The phenomenology of morality would analyse our experiencing of ethical phenomena, and – in Stachewicz's opinion, the phenomenology of Scheler, Nicolai Hartmann,

[9] P. Dybel, *Panie Heidegger...*, op. cit., p. 336.

[10] Cf. K. Stachewicz, *Próba ugruntowania moralności...*, op. cit., p. 99.

[11] Cf. ibidem, p. 105.

Hildebrandt or Roman Ingarden accomplishes this quite decently. However, Heidegger's fundamental ontology would fit within the second part of the ethical project, i.e. in the metaphysics of morality, whose task it is to embed moral phenomena within a certain broader whole, which is being.

And because unveiling the sense of being is the principal cognitive task of Heidegger's entire philosophy, one could say that such research of this embedding in the understanding of being, *ergo* the embedding of ethics, is being practised throughout Heidegger's work. Such an attitude even allows Stachewicz, in the context of ethics, to combine the two phases of this philosopher's thought, rejecting the thesis of their essential otherness.[12] The issue of being – he notes, quite rightly – welds the two main phases of development in Heidegger's philosophy, although one has to note that Stachewicz perceives differences in the approaches of the two phases: activistic emphasis and individualism, i.e. a certain kind of emphasis of authenticity characterising the period of which the culmination was *Being and Time*, and focusing on the historical unveiling of Being ("illumination"), in which man (*Da-sein*, consciousness) only participates, drawing from it the fundamental sources of his sense. The concept of ethos is quite suitable for characterising this developmental phase of Heidegger's thinking, and it is rightly cited by Stachewicz in his work:

> Heidegger values the moral dimension, yet at the same time cannot agree to analysis in the framework of ethics that has sprung from the metaphysics of presence. He attempts therefore the path of *archaic* thinking, the thinking of being in its truth, in the integrality of the whole. The ethical dimension must, by its very essence, belong to this whole. The procedure of *epoché*, which excluded the moral sphere and abolished the opposition of good and evil, revealed its temporariness and enabled the disclosure of "ethicality" in its source-like character. On the other hand it is obvious that a program of thought thus understood will not go beyond certain findings regarding the "foundations," beyond analysis of the rudiments. Ethics in the sense ascribed to it by classic tradition cannot be practised on a foundation of the thinking of being. Dependence on objectivised values and established moral norms would push man into falling, into the rule of *das Man* [the "they" – A.P.]. It would be a sin against the *Eigentlichkeit* [i.e. authentic – A.P.] existence of man. Besides, man properly inhabiting his *ethos* has no need for a world of norms and rules.[13]

[12] A certain type of indication for this otherness is Heidegger's rejection in the period following the "turn" of the fundamental thesis adopted in the period of *Being and Time*, according to which "there is no being without existence, and no existence without being."

[13] K. Stachewicz, *Próba ugruntowania moralności...*, op. cit., p. 101. A position close to Stachewicz's is taken by Jacek Filek in his article *Heideggera ideał egzystencji a materialna etyka wartości* ("Studia Filozoficzne" 2/1989). This Cracow's philosopher of morality emphasises that: (1) fundamental ontology is based on Heidegger's consciously adopted ideal of a proper (though frequently falling) existence, (2) that it is loaded with evaluating definitions (despite a declaration of sticking to pure description)and (3) that despite not providing guidelines for conduct along the lines of a material ethics of value, it can be treated as a kind of formal ethics (proclaiming the ideal of self-fulfilment formally understood and resolved in real terms by listening to the voice

These are positions of interpretation diametrically opposed to one another, and as such their evaluation of some kind is essential. Let us begin perhaps by indicating certain pluses and minuses of each approach. An undoubted strength in Dybel's approach is, above all, the courage of questioning Heidegger's findings, of undermining the legitimacy of his schemas of thinking and their validity in the axiological sphere, including in the ethical sphere. This all occurs through Dybel's independent attempt at achieving a phenomenological understanding and description of the fundamental ethical phenomena of guilt and sense of guilt, and of conscience and a guilty conscience (the voice of one's conscience), and which – in his opinion – Heidegger caricatured. Perhaps a weaker aspect of Dybel's approach is the adoption of powerful assumptions regarding what a phenomenon of ethicality is. Accepting these assumptions is risky because intersubjectivity is recognised here as the sole determinant of the ethical character of our deeds and motivations, due to which we forget (together with Dybel) that care for oneself, for one's good life, for leading it rationally, and for virtues and similar things has, since the very beginnings of ethics, also been an important part of it – including in the Greek world. But even if we leave aside the Greek world as one now quite distant from usspiritually, then let us reach for works more relevant to our modern form of existence, e.g. to Kant's book *Metaphysics of Morals* (1797). We see that an important section of this work, *Metaphysical Aspects of the Theory of Virtue*, is dedicated to "man's obligations towards himself."[14] This unveils a certain constriction carried out by Dybel, with consequences for his adverse appraisal of Heidegger, who after all moves boldly beyond this narrowing as he focuses precisely on man's care for himself.[15]

As for Stachewicz's approach, then a plus of a kind is his significant acquiescence in relation to Heidegger, while not noticing the difficulties appearing in regard to an approach to his work that strives to discover in it elements of ethicality, difficulties that Dybel writes of, but which Stachewicz does not defeat, but avoids.There are also lesser problems, for example the consistent

of one's conscience, by – among other things – overcoming the dictatorship of anonymous public opinion, that "They"). In Filek's opinion, conduct according to the recommendations of authentic existing would boil down to life according to the guidelines of a material ethics of value postulated for example by Hartmann. However, the two philosophers differ, according to Filek, in the relation of the founding: with Heidegger, authenticity precedes general values, while with Hartmann the latter precede authenticity (self-fulfilment). Filek also stresses Heidegger's distance to morality as belonging to the sphere of incorrect existence.

[14] Cf. I. Kant, *Metafizyka moralności*, trans. E. Nowak, Wydawnictwo Naukowe PWN, Warsaw 2005, pp. 287-328 [transl. from the Polish – J. Weber].

[15] At this point let us also recall that care for oneself was the *Leitmotiv*of the late philosophy of Micheal Foucault.

recognition of 'being' written with an "Upsilon" (i.e. as *Seyn*, which is usually translated into Polish using a capital letter: Bycie [Being]) as synonymous with the Greek *etos* would lead to significant interpretational difficulties in regard to "time of the world-picture" (*die Zeit des Weltbildes*) as the time of the fall and waiting for a new event (*Ereignis*) of Being, for its addressing (*Zuspruch des Seyns*). It would rather force us towards optimism, which one does not actually see in Heidegger's later thinking. His late work is a critique of the culture of the times he had come to live in. Only Gianni Vattimo, in referring to Heidegger, attempts to restore our optimism; we would have this self-proclaimed Italian heir to Heidegger to thank for the proper ethical foundation mediated in the philosophy of being.[16] In admitting that Vattimo was right, one would have to state at the same time that Heidegger conducted a mistaken self-interpretation, which happens to be hard to agree to. And as such the equating of being with ethos, as highlighted by Stachewicz, is not convincing. According to Heidegger we are currently living in an age of Being devoid of ethos. We only need to learn how to inhabit the Earth properly. But we cannot achieve this by ourselves; a new Event of Being is essential.

There are of course also interesting aspects to the stance taken by Stachewicz. Among them I would put his attempt at grasping the consequences of the intentions of Heidegger himself, for example the will of rebuilding that whole in which the phenomenon of ethicality is placed, even if this phenomenon has not been satisfactorily worked out phenomenologically. Another positive point in the approach presented by Stachewicz is – I believe – the attempt at putting forward the possibility of two mutually complementary approaches to ethical issues, namely metaphysical and phenomenological, and the theory this entails, that they do not have to fight one another as they can supplement each other perfectly. As we know, Heidegger criticised all philosophy of values, including therefore ethics practised from the point of view of the philosophy of values (Rickert, Scheler and others). Stachewicz strives to rehabilitate it under the name of the phenomenology of morality, while retaining the term metaphysics of morality for Heidegger's position.At the same time he believes that one does not bother the other, one does not rule out the other; on the contrary – these approaches are complementary, cognitively exhausting the entirety that the philosophical description of the ethical phenomenon constitutes.

What conclusions therefore arise from my debate of "correspondence" between Dybel and Stachewicz, in the context of what Heidegger answered to

[16] As an example, let us point here to Vattimo's main work on this topic: *La fine della modernità*, Garzanti Editore, Milano 1985; Polish translation – *Koniec nowoczesności*, transl. M. Surma-Gawłowska, Universitas, Cracow 2006) or *Le avventure della differenza*, Garzanti Editore, Milano 1980.

the student asking him about an ethics? The 'answer' that Heidegger gave to the student is now – it would seem – incidental. Much suggests that it should be interpreted rather as meaning that he believes that *Being and Time* truly does unveil the conditions for the possibility of ethicality, for its foundations. But this is an ethicality understood as authenticity, as the "right," "proper" (genuinely human, one could say) manner of existing, profound and self-aware, for which the existential of determination (*Entschlossenheit*) – the choice of oneself – is constitutive. And this in turn is only possible via the authentic ("proper") form of care, determined by the authentic experiencing of embedding in time ("temporalisation") and a number of other phenomena. But – continuing with such conclusions – Heidegger's mistake was that he narrowed down ethics to care of oneself. Relations to others are reduced to a breaking free of the dictatorship of the anonymous "they" that enslaves us, denying us our authenticity, and especially our responsibility for ourselves.The social or community dimension plays almost no positive role at all in Heidegger's constituting of ethicality in human existence. Taking into account the being-with and co-existing (*Mitsein* and *Mitdasein*) as existentials of existence (the conscious existence) changes little here, as Heidegger's perspective remains existentially-secluding, and extremely individualistic. He is incapable of considering the constitutive role of another/of others in the emergence of my "selfhood." In this sense one could say that if, in line with Stachewicz, *Being and Time* is acknowledged as belonging to the metaphysics of morality, then one would have to say that Heidegger outlines within it only a framework of ethicality at the most. And, we should add here, his sketch is not fully adequate.

These conditions for the possibility of its materialising were grasped perfectly by Czesław Miłosz in his verse dedicated to the sources of ethicality. Entitled*Unde malum? (Where does evil come from?)*, the poem constitutes an answer to Różewicz's verse, a fragment of which Miłosz quotes in his work's motto. This reads as follows: "Where does evil come from?/It comes from man/always from man/only from man" (Tadeusz Różewicz), and Czesław Miłosz answers thus:

Alas, dear Tadeusz
good nature and wicket man
are romantic inventions
you show us this way
the depth of your optimism

so let man exterminate
his own species
the innocent sunrise with illuminate

a liberated flora and fauna
where oak forests reclaim
the postindustrial wasteland
and the blood of a deer
torn asunder by a pack of wolves
is not seen by anyone
a hawk falls upon a hare
without witness

evil disappears from the world
and consciousness with it

Of course, dear Tadeusz,
evil (and good) comes from man.[17]

I think this is an excellent, poetic commentary to what Heidegger achieved, though in a somewhat more philosophical and speculative manner, and only partially discursive, in his *Being and Time* in the aspect of reflection over what enables the materialising of ethical phenomena, in the sense of fundamental distinctions between good and evil. Does this mean that Heidegger contributed nothing to the philosophical consideration of ethics? What I stated just a moment ago shows that this is not necessarily so.

Comments contained in the famous *Letter on humanism* reveal a certain contribution of his in a somewhat more obvious way. They touch on at least two aspects. The first is the revealing, the emerging of ethics from the perspective of Greek ethos. And the second is the critique of ethics created from the transcendental (a priori) perspective of the philosophy of values, and so a critique of Scheler, Hartmann and the neo-Kantians. I shall take the liberty of illustrating these elements with an appropriate and rather large citation:

> If the name "ethics," in keeping with the fundamental meaning of the word *ethos*, should now say that ethics ponders the abode of the human being, then that thinking which thinks the truth of being as the primordial element of the human being, as one who ek-sists, is in itself original ethics. However, this thinking is not ethics in the first instance because it is ontology. For ontology always thinks solely the being in its being. But as long as the truth of being is not thought all ontology remains without its foundation. Therefore the thinking that in*Being and Time* tries to advance thought in a preliminary way into the truth of being characterizes itself as "fundamental ontology." It strives to reach back into the essential ground from which thought concerning the truth of being emerges. By initiating another inquiry this thinking is already removed from the "ontology" of metaphysics (even that of Kant). "Ontology" itself, however, whether transcendental or precritical, is subject to critique, not because it thinks the being of beings and in so doing reduces being to a concept, but because it does not think the truth of being and so fails to recognize that there is a thinking more rigorous than conceptual

[17] Cz. Miłosz, *To*, Wyd. Znak, Kraków 2001, pp. 76-77, http://www.poemhunter.com/poem/unde-malum/ [30.11.2016].

thinking. In the poverty of its first breakthrough, the thinking that tries to advance thought into the truth of being brings only a small part of that wholly other dimension to language. This language even falsifies itself, for it does not yet succeed in retaining the essential help of phenomenological seeing while dispensing with the inappropriate concern with "science" and "research." [...] In the meantime I have learned to see that these very terms were bound to lead immediately and inevitably into error. For the terms and the conceptual language corresponding to them were not rethought by readers from the matter particularly to be thought; rather, the matter was conceived according to the established terminology in its customary meaning. The thinking that inquires into the truth of being and so defines the human being's essential abode from being and toward being is neither ethics nor ontology. Thus the question about the relation of each to the other no longer has any basis in this sphere.[18]

This excerpt shows, I believe, at least two things. Firstly, that it is Heidegger who restores importance to the plane of ethos, which has become blurred in contemporary ethical thinking. Ethical thinking in the modern era has become too atomised, has "adhered" to the autonomous subject, while the dimension of ethos is always thought of after all in relation to a certain community (or at least such is the case with Aristotle). Whether this is exactly the same with Heidegger is an unknown, since Heidegger does not refer to Aristotle, although he does quote Heraclitus, who – he writes – is found by strangers in his home, next to a bread oven, and they are disappointed to find a great thinker in a prosaic pose, "not even busy baking at the stove. He stands there merely to warm himself."[19] So Heraclitus encourages them to draw closer, to enter his cottage, saying as an encouragement: *ethos anthropos daimon*,which – as Heidegger writes – is usually translated as "A man's character is his daimon," but which he himself, following arduous analysis, renders as "the human being dwells, insofar as he is a human being, in the nearness of god."[20]

The place of abode is, for man, space that is open for the presencing of God. This is precisely how Heidegger puts in his subtly elaborated interpretation, but that reference to community is not contained in his concept of ethos, while the reference to abode, to dwelling, is. But then with Aristotle it is evidently about a certain way of life for man in the *polis*. The fact that Heidegger mentioned the significance of ethos is, despite this, a certain value.

As for the critique of ethics developed from a perspective of the philosophy of values by – one may confidentlysay – Heidegger's "older colleagues," then the following quote from the same work is reliable here:

---

[18] M. Heidegger, "Letter on humanism," trans. F.A. Capuzzi, in *Pathmarks*, Cambridge University Press, Cambridge 1998, p. 271.

[19] Ibidem, p. 270.

[20] Ibidem, p. 269. In confirmation of his interpretation Heidegger quotes Aristotle, according to whom Heraclitus addressed his guests thus: "Here too the gods come to presence" (*De pare anim.* V, 654a 17).

> To think against "values" [Heidegger is talking of his own thinking – A.P.] is not to maintain that everything interpreted as a "value" – "culture," "art," "science," "human dignity," "world" and "God" – is valueless. Rather, it is important finally to realise that precisely through the characterization of something as 'a value' what is so valued is robbed of its worth. That is to say, by the assessment of something as a value what is valued is admitted only as an object for human estimation. But what a thing is in its being is not exhausted by its being an object, particularly when objectivity takes the form of value. Every valuing, even where it values positively, is a subjectivizing.It does not let beings: be. Rather, valuing lets beings: be valid – solely as the objects of its doing. The bizarre effort to prove the objectivity of values does not know what it is doing. When one proclaims "God" the altogether "highest value," this is a degradation of God's essence. Here as elsewhere thinking in values is the greatest blasphemy imaginable against being. To think against values therefore does not mean to beat the drum for the valuelessness and nullity of beings. It means rather to bring the clearing of the truth of being before thinking, as against subjectivizing beings into mere objects.[21]

These words clearly demonstrate how difficult it is to remain a follower of Heidegger and at the same time accept the phenomenology of morality, in which after all the concept of value plays a central role. Suffice to recall the title of a book by the well-known Polish phenomenologist, Józef Tischner, *Myślenie według wartości* [which translates as Thinking in Values], to realise this. Stachewicz attempts to bypass this difficulty by showing certain weaknesses or limitations in Heidegger's approach, just as – in another context – Dybel did. In Stachewicz's case this involves demonstrating that the concept of value used by Heidegger is inadequate and entirely different to the concept of value that Hartmann, Scheler and other phenomenologists of morality had in mind.

Thus we have slowly reached the point at which we have acquired the basis for an assessment, for articulating an answer – cautious by its very nature – to this chapter's titular question. It would seem that this answer should be as follows: *Being and Time*, as well as later works in ontology as broadly understood, and especially fundamental ontology – works referring to *Being and Time* – may be considered a kind of foundation of ethics, in the sense in which Stachewicz speaks of it, namely as belonging to the metaphysics of morality and attempting to disclose a certain larger whole or even unity, from which the phenomenon of ethicality is only just emerging. It may, but the question is, is what Heidegger elaborates sufficient for building such a metaphysics of morality? In other words, will a house built on such foundations stand the test of time? And here there are serious doubts. The sources indicated by Heidegger seem, for a start, too narrow – and there are too few of them. Secondly, they are not particularly discursive. The more Heidegger talks about being/Being, remoulding it in all possible ways, the less clear what he actually has in mind is: consummate human existence, or the Absolute determining

[21] Ibidem, p. 265.

the historical eras of the understanding of being. Nevertheless, his Thinking of Being becomes philosophical and susceptible to some kind of further philosophical "processing." He himself might not be bothered by that. After all, he abandoned academic philosophy quite deliberately, accusing it of unavoidable metaphysicality. But can this satisfy the seekers of the metaphysics of morality? Can they take this path?

Even if we acknowledge that in such a unity or totality (which is undoubtedly necessary) one could – in a weak sense – embed the phenomenon of morality, perhaps we have other, alternative concepts that fulfil this role better. As for concepts contemporary with Heidegger, one could mention Ernst Cassirer's symbolic philosophy of culture, or indicate the philosophy of the spirit created by Hegel precisely with such a metaphysics of morality in mind. Both seem to me better in many respects precisely in the role of metaphysics of morality.

It is obvious that no normative ethics may be drawn either from Heidegger's fundamental ontology or his later philosophy, and what is more – in no sense do they contain in-depth analyses of morality as a phenomenon constituting human existence. Even if they touch on it, this is in a far from adequate way, as they portray social life above all from the perspective of that 'they' (the dictate of public opinion, as described by Heidegger in his later years), the importance of which they distinctly devalue. And yet it is obvious that the phenomenon of ethicality is born on the basis of morality as a dependable social institution. This was identified perfectly, as we have seen, by Dilthey. Only together with development, with cultural sublimation and man's individualisation, does this phenomenon of morality, of complying with certain customs and conventions – or one could say norms controlled by the community – transition to a higher plane of ethicality, as a certain attitude regarding motivation, an attitude regarding which the voice of one's conscience begins to play a constitutive role. And so starting from ethicality, and that from ethical authenticity, i.e. from the individual in his search for authentic existence, and the attempt at deriving from this the phenomenon of morality in the fullness of its manifestations, seems to me a misconception.

Heidegger did not create any ethics, despite the appearance of many interesting remarks ethical in character in his *Being and Time*. Such a conclusion, drawn on the basis of our reasoning constituting but a brief report on many years of research, is confirmed in the work of many researchers investigating this issue. For example Daniel O. Dahlstrom states that Heidegger seems convinced that philosophical ethics is a doubtful enterprise. For one cannot tackle the issue of duty independently of what kind of understanding of being we are dealing with. Forgetting about being must lead to an inadequate grasp of the issue of ethics.[22] Then, for example, the transcendental kingdom of values, the point of reference for which is man, becomes but a substitute of metaphysics. The effect of this is insurmountable aporia, characterising the era of "extreme oblivion of being," leading to annihilation of the authentic dimension of ethicality.

That Heidegger did not write an ethics could also be acknowledged as an expression of his ethical naivety. This can be seen for example in his lectures on the practical philosophy of Kant, given in 1930. The first path for demonstrating the possibilities of freedom leads from the third antinomy of reason, considered in *Critique of Pure Reason*, but this is marked by the primacy of natural causality, which it tries to undermine (to limit, *ergo*: *via negativa*). This is why Kant supplements it with a second path – showing freedom as factually realised in an area subject to practical philosophy. He says, unexpectedly, that although freedom is not an empirical concept, it is actually a certain fact. This means that the world of experience is not the same as full reality, i.e. being an object (objectivity) or an attribute of it does not constitute the only possibility of being.

The idea of the factual nature of freedom thus understood constitutes the basis for Heidegger's separation of categories and existentials. The fact of practical freedom must be demonstrable, and not through the experience of a certain object, but through the materialising of practical laws of pure reason. If will – according to Kant – is the ability to act according to one's own presentations (perceptions), then pure will – pure practical reason – means acting according to presentations not drawn from experience but on the basis of motivations deriving from the need for self-definition. Our factual conduct based on the categorical imperative makes the practical (factual) experience of freedom possible for us, which at the same time is an opening of the space of possible ethicality. Because when we project for ourselves the maxims of will, we are conscious not only of its possibility, but also of its factuality.

Therefore pure will, as Heidegger rightly observes, is wanting oneself. However, he does not notice that pure will is not to be found beyond all possibility of uncertainty, doubt and hesitation. This in turn means that referring to habits and customs (and so to the sphere of the "they") – enabling us to define our commitments towards others – may sometimes prove essential. According to Heidegger, the ethicality of action does not mean we are making some kind of value a reality, but that we really do want, i.e. we decide, we

[22] Cf. D.O. Dahlstrom, "Seinsvergessenheit oder moralphilosophische Naivität Heideggers Interpretation der praktischen Philosophie Kants," in *Zur philosophischen Aktualität Heideggers*, D. Papenfuss, O. Pöggeler (eds), Klostermann Verlag, Frankfurt am Main 1991, vol. 1, pp. 161-179.

want in the existential mode of deciding, i.e. we take responsibility, and in this taking we become an existence.

In Dahlstrom's opinion Heidegger is right in observing that pure will thus understood is neither empty nor condemned to transcendental values.

> He is wrong, though, when he imagines that one can totally detach the reality of that wanting from the content of the categorical imperative (i.e. from ethical rules). It is a naivety to believe that what we "really" want can be defined from the very wanting itself. [...] How should such real wanting cross to knowledge of interpersonal duties, for the determination of which Kant introduced the categorical imperative? When one reads in Heidegger, that such real, significant wanting is already in an ethical community with others, the suspicion arises that it derives from the fact of the existence of some kind of peasant or aristocratic morality.[23]

With Heidegger there was no room for ethics either before or after the turn, even though – says Robert Dostal in turn – the question about measurement (of our action) was important for him in both periods.[24] The turn, which really did take place, was not that Heidegger predicted in *Sein und Zeit.* In the planned transition from fundamental ontology to meta-ontology (the ontology of Being), ethics was supposed to appear, which apparently he announced in this Marburg lectures. However, the only germ that could have served as a basis for ethics remained undeveloped, i.e. co-being with others as a fully existential source. Heidegger does not understand in what way interpersonal relations could be significant for answers regarding the fundamental question about being. In his opinion, the metaphysical character of *Da-sein* can never be drawn from man's organisation as a species, from life-with-oneself. At the same time Heidegger forgot that although neither Aristotle nor Plato drew the character of the human being directly from social or political life, both assumed the existence of a community (*polis*) where this character is revealed and shaped.

This can be seen perfectly in the meaning that Aristotle ascribes to friendship. With Heidegger we shall never find room for eros or friendship. He strolls towards the fullness of being through death, fear and existential solitude, and not via friendship or love. He hops from the first person singular (let us recall, for example, his term "always-being-mine") to the first person plural (the "nation"), omitting the personal relationship of Me – You (love, friendship). He doesn't notice Aristotle's hints saying that he who by their nature lives beyond *polis*, is either an evil person or a demi-god (a superhuman). Or perhaps he notices, but opts for man in the position of a demi-god, which may be indicated by the mistaken analogy he makes when comparing his "shepherd of

23 Ibidem, p. 176 [transl. from the Polish – J. Weber].

24 Cf. R.J. Dostal, "Eros, Freundschaft und Politik: Heideggers Versagen," in *Zur philosophischen Aktualität...*, op. cit., vol. 1, pp. 180-196.

Being" with the Platonic statesman (distinguishing features of which are, after all, bravery and moderation).[25]

One could even risk stating that Heidegger's analysis of existence is a certain kind of caricature of the real being-of-people-in-the-world: it accentuates apoliticism and alienation from the social world. The *Da-sein* existence in its factuality is supposed to be a place for the embedding of the issue of sense, including the soundness of ethics, despite it being unable structurally to adequately bear how individual areas of being are born and come into effect.[26] The fact that Heidegger did not undertake in-depth analyses of actions is to a certain extent responsible for this. This is for him but a bold opting for a full existence; theory does not differ from practice in it, because the materialisation of something is not the essence of action for Heidegger. Thinking does not become action because an influence or application derives from it. "Thinking works when it thinks."[27]

Manfred Riedel in turn believes that the "turn" in Heidegger's thinking was a result of him realising that *Sein und Zeit* omits nature as a force independent of the projecting of *Da-sein*, of its sense-creating activity. He relates in this manner to Kant's depiction of nature, but misses its second meaning – seen in Kant – according to which nature is a force independent of man. Here Kant tackles Aristotle's teachings of the unity of φύσις (*physis*) and ἔθος (*ethos*), based on the fact that man distinguishes the possibility of nature transcending, which leads to the possibility of accepting responsibility for its transformation. On the other hand he is a biological being, due to which his *ethos* (demeanour) is a part of the *physis*, as names for all manners of being. Man's *ethos* is expressed by the Heidegger formula of being-in-the-world, understood from the beginning in the sense of dwelling, being familiarised with something, and caring for something.

The hermeneutics of being thus understood is supposed to be a condition of any ontological study. However, in reference to nature it remains undeveloped in *Sein und Zeit*, among other things because the concept of the world that comes into play here is built from the perspective of what surrounds existence, his surroundings (*Uwelt*). The full hermeneutics of factuality is transformed in the direction of *Da-sein* metaphysics, which leads to the ethical phenomenon vanishing from the field of vision.[28] This is surprising as fundamental ontology

[25] Dostal does not see the possibility emerging here. Cf. ibidem, p. 195.

[26] Cf. A. Rigobello, "Heideggers Kritik des Begriffes »Wert« und die praktische Bedeutung von »Eigentlichkeit«," in *Zur philosophischen Aktualität...*, op. cit., vol. 1, pp. 197-206.

[27] Ibidem. Cf. also B. Cullen, "Heideggers Metaontologie und die Möglichkeit einer philosophischen Ethik," in *Zur philosophischen Aktualität...*, op. cit., vol. 1, pp. 207-216.

[28] Cf. M. Riedel, "Naturhermeneutik und Ethik im Denken Heideggers," in *Zur philosophischen Aktualität...*, op. cit., vol. 1, pp. 75-100 (here pp. 88-94).

is developing via the existentially transformed theory of categories, or basically the Kantian idea of embedding morality in the metaphysical equipment of human existence.

It may seem that Heidegger's position leads to a kind of scepticism towards the possibility of broader research into the ethical phenomenon within his philosophy. Yet the motives that guide him are deeper. They are indicated more openly on a few occasions by his student Hans-Georg Gadamer, for example in his essay *On the Possibilities of a Philosophical Ethics*. Therefore, I believe, it would be worth analysing Gadamer's remarks, not only in regard to their significance in their own right, but also in the sense of clarifying the motivations that Heidegger was guided by in deciding not to deliberate in a more developed manner over the issue of ethics.

Yet even if we take Gadamer's remarks into account, it seems beyond a doubt that his deliberations regarding ethics cannot be carried over in full and without loss to the motivations guiding Heidegger, if only because Gadamer starts out from the fact of communication, of dialogue, of conversation, and therefore – from a community, from a certain "Us." Language for him is always the language of conversation (*Gespräch*), and not the language of delivering a speech (*Rede*), a poetic comment that constitutes the world then inhabited by others. As such there is far-reaching otherness here, which also causes reference to other authors. It is not Heraclitus and his *ethos,*as the abode of gods, that are authoritative for Gadamer, but the *ethos*of Aristotle, close to Hegel's category of *Sittlichkeit* (ethicality). What is interesting is that Gadamer complements the Stagirite with consideration of Kant's contribution to ethics, a contribution that takes into account analyses of the phenomenon of morality, culminating in the Kantian categorical imperative that Gadamer interprets in a direction bringing it close to the voice of conscience. These two ethical theories, or should we say these two figures – Aristotle (complemented by Hegel) and Kant – constitute in his opinion only adequate approaches to philosophical ethics, which allow this ethics to deliver in some way on the task it faces.

Chapter 4

Gadamer's Troubles with Ethics

A browse through the ten-volume issue of Hans-Georg Gadamer's *Collected Works* in search of works *explicite* regarding ethics might well leave one with the impression that he shares Heidegger's scepticism about the possibility of constructing a philosophical ethics. Although as time passed the author of *Truth and Method*put ever greater emphasis on the connection between his hermeneutic concept and practical philosophy (especially interpretational practice), the number of treatises dedicated to ethical issues can be counted on one's fingers. They include three essays in volume 4 of his *Collected Works*: *On the Possibility of a Philosophical Ethics* from 1963; *The Ontological Problem of Value*from 1971, and *The Ethics of Value and Practical Philosophy* from 1982. Four other articles that Gadamer decided to include in this volume, in the section on *Problems of Ethics*, could also be included in this group (although they do not actually tackle ethical issues *explicite*), as may individual treatises from other volumes tackling ethical issues in their historical-philosophical aspect.Those in this last group include such as *Plato's Dialectical Ethics* and *The Idea of the Good in Platonic-Aristotelian Philosophy*,[1] recently also translated into Polish.

The assertion that Gadamer negates the sense of the undertaking of philosophical ethics would, however, be highly premature.This Heidelberg philosopher's way of understanding the issue of ethics and his attitude to previous attempts in this area are presented here based mainly on his essay *On the Possibility of a Philosophical Ethics*,[2] written three years after the publication of *Truth and Method.*

[1] Cf. H.-G. Gadamer, *The Idea of the Good in Platonic-Aristotelian Philosophy*, transl. P.Ch. Smith, Yale University Press, New Haven and London 1986.

[2] H.-G. Gadamer, "Über die Möglichkeit einer philosophischen Ethik," in idem, *Gesammelte Werke*, Mohr Siebeck, Tübingen 1987, pp. 175-188. This work will be cited here on the basis

What Gadamer learned from Heidegger's attitude towards philosophical ethical theory[3] led him to begin by posing the fundamental question: what is, and what can be, philosophical ethics? By no means is this question a banal opening address, as Gadamer realises that if – for a start – we adopt the modern concept of theory, and – secondly – we acknowledge that philosophical ethics is the theory of morality, the consequence is the recognition of the possibility of a purely theoretical and objectivised ethical knowledge, irrespective of its application or non-application in interpersonal practice in life. An engineer possesses objectivised knowledge on how to build a bridge, but by no means does he have to build that bridge. The ethicist-philosopher would be in a similar situation: he would possess the knowledge of what is good, right and just, but this would not oblige him to live by the pointers of this knowledge. An example of such an approach is the *casus* of Scheler, who in response to a question posed by students about why he – who unveiled the structure and hierarchy of values – did not live his life in keeping with this knowledge, is said to have asked back: "Does the signpost go in the direction it points?"[4]

For Gadamer such a solution is absolutely unacceptable, as it would mean the unjustified condescension of the philosopher, while paying no heed at all to the ethicality of his own conduct. In his opinion, the error in Scheler's answer results from the fact that philosophical ethics (i.e. the philosophical consideration of morality) is wrongly ascribed the status of pure theoretical knowledge. Gadamer believes that despite general (and therefore theoretical) elements appearing in it, its connection with doing, with action, with the authentication of knowledge with action – and this always in a specific moral situation – denies this knowledge the status of being pure and arbitrarily applied theory. This protects us additionally from adopting the absurd (in Gadamer's opinion) belief in moral progress, supposedly being a result of progress in ethical knowledge.[5] Nicolai Hartman, elaborating on the ideas of Scheler, was on the track of correctly grasping the relation between theory and practice; he believed that ethical knowledge (mainly in the form of a philosophy of values) constructed by the phenomenologists of morality "has [...] a maieutic

---

of the translation by Joel Weinsheimer, *On the Possibility of a Philosophical Ethics* published in *The Gadamer Reader. A Bouquet of the Later Writings*, ed. R.E. Palmer, Northwestern University Press, Evanston 2007.

[3] We use the term "philosophical ethical theory" here to emphasise the different character of such theories from psychological or sociological theories of ethicality, the possibilities of which cannot be questioned if only because "what is factual is essentially possible."

[4] H.-G. Gadamer, *On the Possibility of...*, op. cit., p. 278.

[5] Ibidem, p. 278.

function for the consciousness of moral value; that is, it affords an ever richer explication of the moral, in that it reveals forgotten or unrecognized values."[6]

Therefore philosophical ethics is not "distanced knowledge," but knowledge serving direct practice, and even knowledge that has coalesced with this practice. It is knowledge that co-constitutes the existence of its holder, while this existence conditions the kind of knowledge that harmonises with it. This is why ethical knowledge, the instructions of which nobody wants to live according to, is essentially pseudo-knowledge, it is ostensible knowledge. Ethics understood as "knowledge of the universal," claims Gadamer, "is implicated in the moral questionablenessassociated with the concept of the universal law."[7] Soulless "keeping the law [...] leads to the real sin," as uncompromising, blind obedience to law "prevents [...] from obeying the commandment to love"resulting from the specific situation in which one finds oneself. "The reflexive generality which is necessarily its philosophical métier entangles it in the questionableness of law-based ethics."[8]

Gadamer perceives two paths that, together, allow a way out of this dilemma. The first is represented by Kant's ethics, the second – by Aristotle's. Neither of them can be absolutised, he adds, as only the two together do justice to the possibilities of philosophical ethics. Kant's ethical formalism refers, admittedly, to the concept of law, but this is not law imposed from outside (for example by nature), forcing the individual to comply, but "self-legislation," the sources of which reside in human rationality and human freedom. Gadamer, educated by the neo-Kantians (of Breslau and Marburg), despite ultimately distancing himself from neo-Kantianism (in keeping with Heidegger's reasoning), continued to hold a deep respect for Kant. However, this was more in regard to practical then theoretical philosophy. By breaching the fatalistic determinism of the world via acknowledgement of the "fact of human freedom," Kant had created – in Gadamer's opinion – the foundations for a truly human (as based on autonomy and not heteronomy) theory of morality.

There were many places in his work where Gadamer expressed his admiration for this part of Kant's philosophical legacy, perhaps to the fullest in his treatise *Citizens of Two Worlds*, originally published in the highly-read booklet *Das Erbe Europa* [The Heritage of Europe], 1989). Among other things, he declares that the forming of European [Western] civilization by science implies not only a distinction, but brings with it a profound tension into the modern world. On the one hand, the tradition of our culture, which formed us, deter-

[6] Ibidem, p. 278. Cf. N. Hartmann, *Problem wartości w filozofii współczesnej*, transl. W. Galewicz, in W. Galewicz, *N. Hartmann*, Wiedza Powszechna, Warsaw 1987, pp. 299-308.

[7] H.-G. Gadamer, *On the Possibility of...*, op. cit., p. 279.

[8] Ibidem.

mines our self-understanding by means of its linguistic-conceptual structure which originated in Greek dialectic and metaphysics. On the other hand, the modern empirical sciences have transformed our world and our whole understanding of the world. The two stand side by side.

> That Kant justified both constitutes, in fact, his epoch-making significance. He recognized the boundaries of pure reason, proved their limitation to possible experience, and at the same time he justified the autonomy of practical reason. The limitation of the use of the categories and especially of causality to the appearances given in experience meant, on the one hand, the total justification of the scientific investigation of appearances – even when it concerned life or the social-historical world. On the other hand, however, the limitation of causality to experience is at the same time the justification of practical reason, in so far as its 'causality from freedom' did not contradict theoretical reason.Kant's accomplishment of having justified the priority of practical reason, was then developed by German Idealism to such an extent that this priority conferred its status upon the concept of spirit and all its objectifications in economy and society, law and state. These objectifications are not only appearances and therefore the 'object' of science, but also always intelligible facts of freedom, and that means that their truth can only be obtained in another manner.[9]

At the same time Gadamer notices that this "fact of freedom," manifested ethically in the form of good will – and quoting Kant's well-known comments, that there "is nothing it is possible to think of anywhere in the world, or indeed anything at all outside it, that can be held to be good without limitation, excepting only a good will"[10] – cannot be "objectively" (i.e. intersubjectively) proven. However, it can be subjectively felt by accepting a commitment determined by the situational application of the categorical imperative, which means by proceeding according to a maxim generated in keeping with a priori moral laws. The individual authenticates by living – through their conscious choices, guided not by the desire for pleasure or happiness, but by the vision of universal good – that morality may exist. The existence of freedom, and *ergo* morality, is not the existence of a natural fact but the existence of the ethical man. Referring to Kant's views, Gadamer writes that:

> [...] outside the phenomenal order, where there is only the relation of cause and effect, there exists yet another intelligible order, to which we belong not as sensible but as rational beings and within which the standpoint of freedom, the self-legislation of reason (*Selbstgesetzgebung*), can be rightly understood. That we "ought" is something we know with practical reason's unconditional certainty, which is not contradicted by theoretical understanding. Freedom is theoretically not impossible, and it is practically necessary."[11]

---

[9] Citation from this booklet published in *Hans-Georg Gadamer on Education, Poetry and History*, ed. D. Misgeld and G. Nicholson, transl. L. Schmidt and M. Reuss, State University of New York Press, New York 1992, p. 213.

[10] I. Kant, *Groundwork for the Metaphysics of Morals*, transl. and ed. A.W. Wood, Yale University Press, New Haven and London 2002, p. 9.

[11] H.-G. Gadamer, *On the Possibility of...*, op. cit., p. 280.

Kant, deriving his concept of ethicality from compliance (by one's own will) to the instructions of the categorical imperative, opposing personal inclinations, also set out at the same time on the path of moral rigorism. Good deeds performed for the pleasure drawn from their doing are, in his opinion, beyond the area of ethicality. On the other hand, though, Kant was far from ascribing moral superiority to somebody justifying their deeds philosophically over somebody who fulfils their duties guided by the simple awareness of obligation. The need for ethical deliberation does not result in Kant seeing – as Gadamer puts it – "moral philosophy [...] transcending the law-creating simplicity of the simple consciousness of duty." It results solely from the fact that the "innocence of the simple heart" occasionally succumbs to wavering, to temptations, and is ready to stray from the path of justice. The task for practical reason is to steer it back to the right path, and the categorical imperative – the formal character of which does not violate the situational character of the duty – constitutes an appropriate basis for this.

Gadamer evidently sees the essence of Kantian ethical reflection, and at the same time its greatest contribution, in its attempt to grasp the forming of ethical awareness. In this respect he writes that: "[...] Kant's rigor – where the only cultivated will that possesses moral value is the one that acts purely out of duty and against all inclination – has a clear methodological significance."[12] A person making the effort of ethical consideration has *de facto* already acknowledged the existence of moral law. Gadamer considers the readiness for such consideration close in essence to an examination of conscience, while the categorical imperative would only have to teach the preclusion of all elements deriving from inclination, contaminating our ethical consideration. However, in his opinion this fundamentally proper approach has a certain defect. The methodical contrasting of obligation and inclination makes it difficult for Kantian ethics to recognise the fact of the building of ethical character (meaning the creation of a kind of "inclination to do good," as a kind of habit), constituting as it were a "side effect" of measures undertaken in keeping with the recommendations of the categorical imperative. This in turn leads to the incomplete embracing of the phenomenon of moral awareness.

"The truth of moral consciousness," states Gadamer, "lies not merely in the scrupulousness with which it continually tries to become tortuously conscious of impure motives and inclinations. Of course there are occasions of conflict when such moral self-examination takes place. Conscience, however, has no permanent *habitus*; instead it is something by which we are struck, by which we are awakened. And how? Isn't there such a thing as a "broad" con-

[12] Ibidem, p. 281.

science? In can hardly be denied that the wakefulness of conscience depends upon orders of substance in which one always already lives. The autonomous moral reason, therefore, assuredly has the character of intelligible self-determination; but that does not exclude the fact that all human action and decision are conditioned by experience."[13]

This is why Kant's exceptionally valuable deliberations need to be supplemented by consideration of the conditioning of morally valuable deeds. Hegel raised this factor in his critique of Kant's ethics from the point of view of his concept of ethicality as decorum (*Sittlichkeit*). "Isn't he right," asks Gadamer rhetorically, "when he discerns the essence of ethics (*Sittlichkeit*) not in the self-necessity of an imperative ethics, but in the ethos (*Sitte*) – that is, in the substantiality of the moral order that has its embodiment in the great objectivities of family, society and state?"[14]

Long before Hegel this path was set out by Aristotle, in whose ethical contemplations Gadamer perceives an alternative and supplement to Kantian research into the essence of morality. A brief – partially critical, partially apologetic – response to the assertions of the material ethics of value, created in clear opposition to Kantian formalism by Max Scheler and Nicolai Hartmann, constitutes a sort of transition for Gadamer. He perceives its unquestionable merit in the fact that it made not the forms of duty and will the object of philosophical-ethical analyses, but the substantive contents of morality. Focusing on the concept of value, moving into the forefront here, signified a break with the supporting of morality on duty, and therefore its "narrow focus [...] on the mere goals of effort and the norms of the Ought."[15]

Scheler's ethical reflection, transcending the aspirations of pure moral will towards direct analysis of the awareness of value, reaches downwards towards the sphere of life values and practical values. "Such an ethics," claims Gadamer, "really comprehends the substantive contents of morality, not just the reflective phenomenon of the reason that tests [ethical – A.P.] laws."[16] However, the material ethics of value has major limitations that command one to seek other solutions. These limitations are:

(1) the difficulty of taking into account the concept of ethos and its historical transformations, resulting from the a priori character of research into axiological awareness conducted by Scheler and his successors; and

(2) adopting the pure, transcendental subject as the point of reference for this research and its findings.Both these limitations are a result of the assumptions of Scheler's phenomenology.

[13] Ibidem, p. 282.

[14] Ibidem.

[15] Ibidem, p. 283.

[16] Ibidem.

Although he rightly diagnosed that "[...] every morality is a concrete ethical form,"[17] he was not – in Gadamer's opinion – capable of taking this into account in his comprehensive philosophical (axiological) construct. It was only Nicolai Hartmann who drew the right conclusion from this, recognising that the task of moral philosophy is not to lecture anybody, for example by setting new and previously unknown tables of values. Its role is only to develop an awareness of values, the discovery of values one was previously unaware of. Therefore it has a maieutic function: influencing the individual ethos via the never-ending rectifying of the awareness of values. And he who based his ethical concept on the notion of ethos was, of course, Aristotle. Gadamer sees a restoration of the validity of Aristotle's insights as the greatest chance for overcoming the limitations of the Kantian position.

In amending the one-sidedness of the Socratic-Platonic "intellectualism," Aristotlestates that moral conduct is not solely an effect of ethical reflection. He also takes account in his reflections of the dependency of concrete decisions on the practical and social conditions in which they are realised. By doing so he manages to do justice to both sides or aspects of ethicality: the subjective and the substantive. As Gadamer writes: "[...] in rendering the nature of moral knowledge so clear that (under the concept of "choice of") it covers just as much the subjectivity that judges in the case of conflict as the substance of law and custom which determines its moral knowledge and its particular choices. His analysis of *phronesis*recognizes that moral knowledge is a way of moral being itself, which therefore cannot be prescinded from the whole concretion of what he calls ethos."[18]

According to Gadamer, Aristotle manages to save in ethics what is general, without its unnecessary absolutisation to a form of a priori moral law. Moral laws exist, but they have the form of something that has been defined by the term *legomena*, of historically set human generalisations, based on the learning flowing from analysis of what human action is. It is by no accident that Gadamer reiterates here – also by way of explaining the absence of ethical deliberations in Heidegger – this assertion, according to which "For a long time we have not considered the essence of action decisively enough."[19] This is why – emphasises the Heidelberg hermeneutist– in the key category of his ethics, meaning in the concept of phronesis, Aristotle recognises a certain kind of moral existence "immersed" in the ethos.

[17] Ibidem, p. 283.

[18] Ibidem, p. 284.

[19] Ibidem, p. 278. This assertion comes from the famous *Letter on humanism*. In the edition cited in the previous chapter (*Pathmarks*) a slightly different translation of it is to be found on p. 239: "We are still far from pondering the essence of action decisively enough."

Moral knowledge, prudence or in other words *phronesis*, employs logic deduction when the requirement (i.e. what should be done) revealing itself in a concrete situation "[...] is related to what is considered right and proper in general."[20] But this is not the ordinary logic of subsumption, because it is on the existence of man, on his spiritual constitution, and therefore on his ethical moulding that whether he makes an attempt at all at such deduction and whether he does so properly depends. For example this will not be done by somebody who is "overwhelmed with emotion." Aristotle ties the proper identification of what, in a given situation, "should be done" with *hexis*, with *habitus*, with adopting a certain attitude or achieving a "lasting disposition" for acting in a particular manner and not some other. Gadamer emphasises that the fundamental fact that moral action – for a start – depends to a greater degree on our existence (way of being, existential choice) than on our "distinct consciousness" (*eidos*), and – secondly – this action co-creates this manner of existing, most often strengthening and intensifying it and at times achieving a breakthrough in it, did not escape the attention of this Greek genius.

Taking into account the entirety of the subjective and non-subjective conditionings of our moral actions in his concept of *phronesis*, Aristotle had to relate individual ethics to social ethics; he had to correlate them. The outcome of this is the finding that – as Gadamer rightly concludes – "ethics proves to be a part of politics,"[21] as our actions "are situated within the horizon of the *polis*,"[22] a form of life that situates our individual existence within what is shared, and so for which we are also permanently jointly responsible. This is precisely why friendship, which Gadamer situates "[...] as that mean between virtues and goods,"[23] becomes such an important object of Aristotelean ethical consideration. As we shall find out in the chapter on the ethical research of Ricoeur, this French hermeneutist also attributes friendship a key position in the renewal of philosophical ethics that is meant to occur via a joining of Aristotle and Kant, a critical connection, i.e. the kind that extracts from their concept the right insights, ones that can be retained today as well, while at the same time rejecting mistaken diagnoses.

The depth in Aristotle's approach was defined by Gadamer as "speculative depth"; above all the German philosopher sees it in his brilliant intuition of the manifold consolidation of our deeds. The diagnosis that Aristotle proposes also provides an answer to a question "tormenting" Gadamer, on "how a philosophical ethics, a human doctrine of the human, is possible without

20 Ibidem, p. 284.

21 Ibidem, p. 286.

22 Ibidem.

23 Ibidem, p. 287

requiring a superhuman self-transcendence."[24] According to the author of *Truth and Method*, Aristotle resolves this by not treating ethics as general knowledge in the full meaning of this word, as a theory that would be indifferent towards its practical, situational application. "The universal, the generic," asserts Gadamer, "that can be expressed only in a philosophical inquiry [...] is in fact not essentially different from what guides the usual, completely untheoretical sense of norms present in every deliberation on moral practice."[25]

Philosophical ethical consideration is an element of moral knowledge, which – guiding our actions as good-orientated – is at the same time an element of our moral existence (ethical existence). *Phronēsis*, as ethical prudence, is ἀρετή (*arete*) – a trait of character (*ergo*: of existence) of the person possessing (manifesting) it. "It is not," writes Gadamer, "something for anyone and everyone, but only for those whose education in society and state has brought their own being to a point of such maturity that they are capable of recognizing general rules of thumb in concrete perplexities (*Betroffensein*) and putting them into practice."[26] This means: for it to become a pointer for the actions that should proceed in keeping with this diagnosis. Phronesis is not possessed by he who only theorises, who supposedly identifies what should be done in a given situation but does not do so, out of fear, convenience, or egocentrism. This is also why the philosopher-moralist does not hold any automatically-deserved superiority over an ordinary person undertaking the everyday effort of making ethical decisions. By thus laying out this issue, "Aristotle too distanced himself from all false claims incident to the idea of a philosophical ethics."[27]

The supplementing of the Kantian and Aristotelean approach in the portrayal presented – or rather sketched – by Gadamer, then comes across rather incongruously, at first glance even bringing to mind a certain contradiction. "Whereas Kant," states the author of *Truth and Method*, "[...] by releasing the unconditional practical reason from all the conditionedness of human nature and presenting it in transcendental purity, Aristotle [...] places the conditionedness of human life at the center [...]."[28] Yet both considered the support of ethical behaviour the main task, in which philosophical ethics may only support the concretion of generality, its application in a specific situation. Kant's merit lies, in Gadamer's opinion, in revealing the absence of purity in moral deduction, i.e. in indicating the necessity of freeing oneself from the medley of moral and non-moral motives. However, he introduced another important

[24] Ibidem.

[25] Ibidem.

[26] Ibidem, p. 288.

[27] Ibidem.

[28] Ibidem.

aspect of the issue: the conditioning of any human existence and any usage of reason. As a result he missed the significance that upbringing has in the shaping of ethical existence.

Anybody who has encountered Gadamer's hermeneutic theory knows what enormous importance he ascribes to the category of *Bildung* in hermeneutic experience, which should be understood as shaping within the individual an openness toward manifestations of reality as yet unknown to them (for example art, religion, and literature). So no surprise that an emphasis of the significance of this category crowns Gadamer's deliberations over the tasks of philosophical ethics. It would seem the Gadamer took over the category of education/formation from Hegel, in whose phenomenology of the spirit it is known to play a central role.[29] Gadamer cleanses it admittedly of the longings for the Absolute, and claims towards absolute knowledge, at the same time emphasising the significance that upbringing (together with self-instruction) has for man's spiritual existence. In his opinion Kant disregarded this, unduly emphasising that the application of pedagogical means of reward and punishment in moral upbringing could miss the goal, consolidating and intensifying egoistic – and therefore unethical (non-ethical) – impulses in the pupil. However, discerning this concern cannot lead to one overlooking the fundamental fact that "exemplar and imitation (*Nachfolge*), along with the ground of solidarity, sympathy, and love [...] form the 'ethos' of humankind prior to all appeals to reason and thus make such appeals possible in the first place [...]."[30]

And it is precisely this, according to Gadamer, that constitutes the essence of Aristotle's ethics. Kant belittles it, perceiving within it only the danger of a mingling of ethical and non-ethical motivations. But after all, claims the Heidelberg philosopher, "in particular, ancient *eudaimonia* [...] cannot be accused of heteronomy. [...] Aristotle too does not for a moment overlook the fact that people are concerned with justice for its own sake [...]."[31] The determinants of our ethical prudence are not its limitation but a condition of it being possible. Despite the fact that every one of us – for example as a child of their age – is "dependent on the ideas of their time and world, but from this follows neither the legitimacy of moral scepticism nor the exercise of political power in the form of technical manipulation of opinion."[32]

Gadamer does not elaborate on this theme. Nevertheless, it is clear that a more general thesis of his hermeneutics, requiring one to treat with a certain distance any attempts at incorporating this concept into postmodernism, is

[29] Cf. G.F.W. Hegel, *Phänomenologie des Geistes*, Suhrkamp, Frankfurt am Main 2008.

[30] H.-G. Gadamer, *On the Possibility of...*, op. cit., p. 288.

[31] Ibidem, pp. 288-289.

[32] Ibidem, p. 289.

manifested in the rejection of scepticism and relativism. The idea of historical reason (i.e. the historicity of the moulding of human reason) and the related central place for tradition (i.e. the historical message, the *Überlieferung*) do not admit any postmodernist arbitrariness along the lines of *anything goes*. Yet this does not mean that Gadamer is blind to transformations or is a conservative hostile to them. Nevertheless, he does believe that:

> The alterations that transpire in morals and modes of thought that, especially for the elderly, portend the utter dissolution of all morals, come to pass upon an enduring basis. Family, society, and state determine the essential constitution of the human being, in that its ethos replenishes itself with varying contents. Of course, no one knows how to predict what might become of humankind and all its forms of communal life – yet this does not mean that everything is possible, that everything is directed by arbitrariness and caprice and can be determined by the powers that be. There are things that are naturally right.[33]

In the final fragment of his essay on the tasks of philosophical ethics, following on from this confession, Gadamer once again recalls Aristotle and his teacher Plato, according to whom: "the system of being is powerful enough to set limits to all human confusion."[34] However, there is no doubt that in referring to family, society and state as a certain type of "lasting" moral order, he is referring *implicite* to Hegel. Hegel is known to have based his theory of ethicality on the triad of family, civic society, and state, assigning each of these elements a separate task within the shaping of man's ethicality. Today, when the traditional function of the family is being widely challenged, and when the significance of state is questioned, while civic society, already a threat to morality for Hegel, is "pushing and shoving," occupying the entire space of social existence, this gives rise to the justified question of how – in these new conditions – can Hegel's and Gadamer's hope for the harmonious moulding of the individual in a world dominated by egoistic rivalry on the social agora achieve fulfilment.[35]

Gadamer does not provide a direct answer to this question. The direction of a possible answer, based on his hermeneutic theory, would – it would seem – be set by his unwavering conviction that both family and state will break free of the crisis they have fallen into, once again becoming the foundation of an all-embracing and pro-societal moulding of the human individual. But what about the source of morality if this is not to come about? If the nation state, bonded by a community of history and culture, manifested in a community

[33] Ibidem.

[34] Ibidem.

[35] I write about the significance and topicality of Hegel's conception of ethicality (against a background of harmonious structure of society) in an issue of the Cracow journal *Principia* dedicated to Hegel (*Hegel jako teoretyk i krytyk społeczeństwa obywatelskiego*).

of speech, passes into history, eliminated by supranational ways of organising humankind (of the kind of the European Union in its form desired by some)? If the traditional family, as the place of original acculturation, "goes broke," yielding to creations simulating it or entirely ceding its child-raising tasks to society (e.g. the crèche-to-nursery-to-school system that we know)?

These questions, in relation to the hope placed in Hegel's model, provoke one to investigate how the phenomenon of morality was approached by Gadamer's great rival (though also his ally) and at the same time joint-creator of modern hermeneutic philosophy, Paul Ricoeur. We shall have a closer look at his ethical theory in the next chapter.

Beforehand, though, let us carry out a brief recapitulation of Gadamer's approach to ethics resulting from his understanding of hermeneutics. This approach was a derivative of his view of practical philosophy in general, a view for which Aristotle's contribution remains constitutive. In his work *The Idea of the Good in Platonic-Aristotelian Philosophy*, Gadamer asserts that Aristotle developed his thinking about*praxis* in his unveiled critique of the position taken by his master, Plato, a critique regarding the abstractionism and constructivism characterising Platonic thinking of the good, the state, and ethics. "Thus the overall result of our investigation is as follows: in basing the question about being on the physei onta and not on the universality of the *eidos* or mathematical-eidetic configurations, Aristotle did indeed subject Plato's teachings to a radical critique. But in the end did he not carry out what Plato intended to do – indeed, even go beyond it in fulfilling it?"[36] However, he did *implicite* accomplish Plato's intention in another, better manner. He reached the conclusion that good is concretised in people's actions and defined only by practical reason. This in turn is based on the concept of goal, which should be restored in its pertinent meaning and extent. Every existence is 'good' when it fulfils its *telos*. Aristotle already defines the teleological cause as the 'cause of good' in his *Metaphysics* (A3 984b1).

However, in order to understand the depth of the move taken by Aristotle compared with Plato, then according to Gadamer one has to realise the essence of practical philosophy. One must not think from the perspective of *techne*, a collection of axiologically neutral regulations serving to achieve something, to accomplish some kind of goal that is "beyond good and evil" in the ethical understanding of these terms. Despite the fact that Aristotles' assertions within his practical philosophy are of a general nature, and as such are *nolens volens* theoretic in character, they are not applied e.g. in the process of generating technical rules. In clarifying this, Gadamer states that: "[...] practical philosophy

[36] H.-G. Gadamer, *The Idea of the Good...*, op. cit., p. 177.

is not a theoretical science in the modern sense – a theoretical science, that is, which might be applied to practice in the way one puts pure natural science to use in [applied – A.P.] medical science. Practical philosophy is rather more like knowledge of cures, and accordingly Aristotle often draws comparisons with this kind of knowledge."[37]

The task or even the goal of practical philosophy is to help those practicing or quoting it to cope with the demand of the moment. "The right thing to do – which one decides on the basis of reasonable, practical deliberation – is not simply a case or instance of a rule. For example, the general structure of *arete* that Aristotle elaborates – namely, to be the mean between two extremes – is not a rule that can be applied. The point of his doctrines is not that one has to hold to the golden mean, but that one oughtto be aware of what one is actually doing when one does what is right. Extremes are always recognizable here, and a clear consensus exists that they should be rejectedwhereas what is right as we know, cannot be definitively specified as such."[38]

Practical reason (*phronesis*) contains not only a double path, whereby on the one hand it has to concretise the general principles that it possesses, while on the other it must generalise its concrete experiences to a form of general principles, and through this my concrete, individual ethical decisions and actions may define with greater precision, define anew and even revise the said principles. In addition it contains something akin to sticking to certain principles, abiding by them, which is not after all an effect of the syllogistic act of deduction. It is this – says Gadamer, quoting Aristotle – that distinguishes somebody prudent, reasonable (φϱόυιμος *phronimos*) from somebody who is only clever (*deinos δεινός*).[39]

This is tied to the next attribute of ethical (practical) wisdom, distinguishing it from technical knowledge: there is no certain way of conveying it to somebody, of teaching it to somebody, if he who is being taught does not project within himself an attitude in life that opens him to this dimension of existence. This attitude is not formed through compelling logical reasoning, but rather through the force of example flowing from others we consider figures of authority, beacons (or people acknowledged as such). And this means from social *ethos*. At the same time the "pupil" must be aware that learning certain ethical principles does not guarantee the will or the skill of their specific application, and does not release him of responsibility for his decisions,

[37] Ibidem, p. 161. In regard to the relations of *techne, theoria* and *praxis* compare Gadamer's article "Teoria, technika, praktyka" (transl. A. Przyłębski), in my book *Gadamer*, Wiedza Powszechna, Warsaw 2007, pp. 213-239).

[38] H.-G. Gadamer, *The Idea of the Good...*, op. cit., p. 163.

[39] Cf. ibidem, pp. 165-166.

responsibility that is essentially responsibility for himself (for his "good life," or – as Heidegger might say – for the Self). "But insofar as the world of human practice is located within the entirety of what exists, the whole sphere of human *praxis*(action) and *poiesis* (doing) has its place within the realm of nature. Not only art imitates nature. Human practice doesso too insofar as it aims for nothing other than the highest fulfillment of human existence itself."[40]

Practical reason is reason referred to *ethos*, it is historical reason constituted by tradition, culture and social development. Such reason does not need justification on the part of philosophical reflection: it constitutes support for the latter. This does not signify a rejection of the possibility of critique or indifference towards critical rationality. It is rather about the curbing of its overstated claims, about a reminder that even if here and there disharmony may appear between what exists and what should be, this does not signify an unsurmountable abyss between the kingdom of existence and the realm of duty, because our social existence is filled with normative elements that we assimilate – sometimes rebelling against them – during upbringing, acculturation, self-formation and actions within a community of fundamentally free people. The centre of gravity of Gadamer's hermeneutic-ethical deliberations lies in the function of mediating between the *logos* and *ethos*, "between the subjectivity of knowledge and the substantiality of existence."

And this is why – as Udo Tietz rightly asserts –

> [...] you can agree with Gadamer when he emphasises the shaping of understanding and valuing via belonging to a particular tradition of some kind of linguistic-cultural community. Neither is the ethics of discourse capable of questioning the hermeneutic insight into the dependence of our understanding and valuing on each understanding of the world. The question about whether and how, in relation to such a particular understanding of the world, a rational justification of universal norms is possible, is naturally not yet answered here.[41]

It so happens that the important and apt remark veiled within this last sentence is to become the inspiration for the hermeneutic ethical concept worked on by Ricoeur.

---

[40] Ibidem, p. 172.

[41] U. Tietz, *Hans-Georg Gadamer zur Einführung*, Junius Verlag, Hamburg 1999, p. 119. [transl. from the Polish – J. Weber].

Chapter 5

Paul Ricoeur's Project for a Hermeneutical Ethics

Paul Ricoeur (1913-2005), the second main representative of hermeneutic philosophy alongside Gadamer, is the author of several dozen works and hundreds of scholarly papers. Their subject-matter is related to his philosophical development, progressing – putting it in a simplified form – from the hermeneutics of symbol, and via the hermeneutics of text and the hermeneutics of action, to the hermeneutics of the human existence. To the latter he dedicated his excellent work *Oneself as Another*, relating productively to Heidegger's analysis of Being-oneself (in *Being and Time*), and critically – to an apologia on the pure subjectivity in transcendental philosophy (Descartes, Kant, Fichte and Husserl) on the one hand, and a rejection of the category of subject in concepts proclaiming the "death of man" (e.g. by Michel Foucault) on the other.[1] Ricoeur dedicates a significant part of his "critical apologia of the subject," which – I believe – will gain the status of a classic in the future, to matters of ethics. The context for the elaboration of his own hermeneutical ethics is created for him by reflection over what Being-oneselfmeans, i.e. what the conditions are for sensing one's own identity in relation to the passage of time, applying to both our *physis* and our *psyche*.

What is this "self"? Why does Ricoeur stop speaking of the ego, of self-knowledge, awareness, the subject (empirical or transcendental)? This French hermeneutist is not inclined to disregard the critique of subjectivity of the 20th century (starting from Nietzsche and Sigmund Freud, via French

[1] P. Ricoeur, *Oneself as Another*, transl. K. Blamey, University of Chicago Press, Chicago and London 1992.

structuralism, to Foucault), subjectivity acknowledged to this day as something incontrovertible, given in direct reflection, and as such constituting a type of essential assumption of intersubjectively binding knowledge (Husserl, Kant, Fichte). However, neither is he prepared to abandon the idea of subjective identity, as unwanted ballast that nobody needs. This is because he believes, not without reason, that this would clash with our experience of ourselves. Experience in which our personal identity constantly manifests itself. In contemplating over how this could be grasped philosophically while assuming that the rejection of the substantial subject is justified, Ricoeur – firstly – introduces the distinction into *idem* ("objective") identity and *ipse* ("subjective") identity, and – secondly – in his masterly analyses of the constituting of *ipse* identity he unveils the significance of communication, of action, of narrative and ethicality – issues acknowledged until then as of secondary importance when discussing this problem.

The *idem* identity type is understood as the identity of our sentient, physical body, which undergoes transformation in every second of our lives, yet is still perceived by us as constantly the same, as our body. *Ipse* identity on the other hand is the identity of one's inner life, the feeling that the I who did something yesterday or a week ago is the same I who is ashamed of whom I am proud today. It is therefore the feeling of unity and continuity linked to our spiritual and mental life. Ricoeur depicts this unity from the perspective of action. For his description of being-oneself ("selfhood"), action is as fundamental in character as is being for Heidegger's *Dasein:* it is not that man is, but that man becomes, and achieves self-knowledge not via contemplation of his own transcendental Self, but through analysis of the actions of which he may be called the author or co-author. This is also why Ricoeur believes that we reach self-recognition not through an a priori existential analysis (in the kind of Heidegger's hermeneutics of *Dasein*), but in a roundabout way: via analysis of acts of communication (conversation), in which we take part, and in which we articulate ourselves, via actions in which we accomplish something and through stories of our lives gathering this into a oneness.

In order to avoid the frequently misleading talk of the subject, Ricoeur introduces the somewhat artificial term "*soi*" to signify such an individual feeling of identity, corresponding to Heidegger's "Selbst" (the self), translated by the Polish translator as "ten-który-jest-sobą," which could be given in English as "he-who-is-himself." This he-who-is-himself is first and foremost he who takes action. Being able to take action becomes here the condition for the possibility of being-oneself ("selfhood"). What is of exceptional importance here is that Ricoeur – just like many other representatives of hermeneutics – rejects the dogmatism of Hume's dichotomy of existence and duty, of description and norm (command).[2] This dichotomy, he says, does not apply to human existences, because the fact that they function according to regulations (commands) belongs to the description of their existence.

The natural transition from description to giving regulations is what narrative constitutes. Not all regulations are ethical in character, of course. However, the concept of narrative identity allows a broadening of the sphere of practical reason such that it steps beyond the scope of simple actions described in analytical theories of action. Human actions, grasped in their entire causative-motivational complexity, are thereby so highly processed in narrative fictions that they abound in anticipations of a moral character, thus building a transition to a *stricte* ethical area. There is no need to add here that a condition for such understanding is rejection of the explanation of human actions in terms of simple causative connections, and therefore the necessity of introducing a different kind of causality: causality from motivation, from self-assessment, from a reference to values experienced (and not only imposed). In order to grasp this motivational source it is essential to pertain to what is different: in me, in another person, in the world. This is tied to Ricoeur's emphasis (in many of his earlier works) of the meaning of what Heidegger named "throwness" (*Geworfenheit*), and Gadamer "effective history" (*Wirkungsgeschichte*) – an immersion in culture, i.e. the necessity of grasping oneself through objectivities (such as language games or social practices), which he-who-is-himself does not generate, but in which he has a share, while they shape him.

Being-oneself thus understood eliminates the threat of solipsism: I am myself, but also you, and he. This concept guarantees a (formal) universality without lapsing into a formal void: every self (the French *soi*) is fulfilled otherwise, is unique. Being-oneself is also being-a-person, in the "weak" understanding of this term formed by Scheler, according to which we are not so much always people in advance, e.g. as representatives of the species *homo sapiens* or as creations of God, as we become such, and so we can cease to be them, descending into a pre-person existence. So here as well action is constitutive: he-who-is-himself indicates himself as the doer of the action, i.e. he takes responsibility for it. Acting, so to speak, signifies – or means – oneself. And therefore, one is oneself not because of possessing a certain substantial foundation (of the type of the immortal soul), but thanks to being able to act in a human manner.

Because of the diversity of actions in which man is embroiled, it would be hard – notes the French philosopher with good reason – to give a good definition of action. Ricoeur therefore opts against doing so, making do with

[2] Ibidem, p. 169.

Wittgenstein's "family resemblance'" because – as he says – there is no single universal model of action. The diversity of types of action results in the *who?* (the subject) of an action frequently having a different sense: therefore the oneness of being-oneself is not given, but is assigned: it is a matter of attestation (of oneself by deed). Selfhood therefore has the character of a task, the character of a project, since the concept of action embraces the notion of "initiating something new": accomplishing goals involving the transcending of purely natural causality towards a motivational, teleological causality.[3]

Man's actions are accompanied by the capacity to experience actions: to undergo influence, to experience something, and as such passivity, particularly evident in the case of suffering. The two sides to an action, the active and the passive, are inseparable. One can also see immediately that Ricoeur's consideration of experience, as essentially belonging to the self, immediately introduces with it the corporeality of human existence. There is no need for artificial constructs ordering us to acknowledge it. He also introduces the presence of other people who in some way or another influence us. Because our own body is also sometimes for us something that is different, the dialectic of selfhood and otherness emerges, and that in the function of a source.

Ricoeur's acknowledgement that psychophysical identity (*idem*), which he identifies with possessing character set in the brain/mind, is not constant but may be subject to subtle changes due to the influence of spiritual identity (*ipse*), is original. The latter has the character of a (thrown) project, based on the capacity of action, i.e. the bringing into existence of something previously not existing, something new. *Idem* (character, psychophysical conditioning) determines – in Ricoeur's opinion – the possible projects, while these in turn have a secondary influenceon the character, altering it. The unpredictability of events related to the realisation of any such project results in the individual's life being a synthesis of continuity and discontinuity: bold projects and their expected consequences interrupt the calm continuity guaranteed by psychophysical identity (character). Only action, and the taking of responsibility for it – which is given by German philosophy as *Selbstbeschreibung als Selbstzuschreibung*: "describing-oneself" as "attributing-to-oneself" – by creating a story of one's own life, helps in restoring momentarily lost identity. This is because the unity of *ipse* only exists as a told (narrative) unity, which leads Ricoeur to posit the theory that the sense and unity of life are a matter of interpretation, and that subjectivity as being-oneself is never given as a certainty.[4] It is fragile. And it only becomes stronger when joined by actions of an ethical character.

---

[3] Ibidem, *Third Study, An Agentless Semantics of Action*, pp. 56-87.

[4] Ibidem.

As has already been said, right from the outset Ricoeur rejects the adequacy of access to the self through self-reflexion, through analysis of self-awareness. A person becomes himself in acts turned towards what is different to him: in comments to another person, in actions addressing the social and natural world, in tales about oneself introducing a narrative unity into the individual's life. It is the sphere of ethicality that creates the highest form of such self-attestation. Deliberation over how this happens allows Ricoeur to develop an original ethical theory capable of reconciling two fundamental yet rival ways in philosophical ethics of approaching the issue of morality. At first Ricoeur divides them, assigning them the terms "ethics" and "morality," in order to unite them in an original though complex theoretical construct, helping us better understand the diverse meanders of ethical life.

This French hermeneutist is aware that in assigning the term "ethics" to the teleological type of moral reflection (Aristotle), and the term "morality" to the deontological type of moral reflection (Kant) he is proceeding arbitrarily (and against tradition). But this is important for him, because it helps overcome the opposition of these two fundamental types of moral reflection, types that cannot be reduced to the other, heading (1) in the direction of their amalgamation into a single whole and (2) their combining with the theory of action (especially with the narrative theory of action), which in turn makes it possible for him to (3) challenge Hume's tradition proclaiming the unsuitability of the order of existence and order of duty.[5]

In connection with the above, Ricoeur states the following (which he then attempts to demonstrate):

a) ethics takes priority over morality;

b) the ethical aim (understood as aspiring for a good, fulfilled life) must pass through the filter that ethical norms constitute;

c) in the event of a conflict of ethical norms, recourse to ethics (in the sense as adopted above) is essential.

In understanding ethics as an aspiration for a good, fulfilled life (in tune with the essence of man), while treating morality as the subordination of human actions to universal moral norms, Ricoeur reaches the conclusion that although morality constitutes a certain limitation, it is at the same time essential for the fulfilling of the ethical aspiration. As for recourse at a moment of conflict between moral norms to the ethics of the good life, this means that ethics – as understood here – embraces morality (and without it is not complete).

The connection between the teleological moment and deontological moment can already be found at the level of the predicates ("good" or "duti-

[5] Ibidem, p. 171.

ful") applied to actions, yet it also has its equivalent at the level of "marking oneself": in self-esteem and self-respect. However, self-esteem is something more fundamental than self-respect; esteem for oneself takes on the form of respect for oneself thanks to the prevalence of a norm; self-esteem becomes the backbone of self-respect in a situation where there is no certain norm serving as a dependable guide for having respect for oneself. Every person's growth (as in development of being oneself) culminates in self-assessment and the respect for oneself related to this.[6]

Ricoeur accepts that the ultimate purpose of human actions (i.e. the purpose of purposes) is realisation of the vision of a worthy, "fulfilled life." As such, it is the "good life" that constitutes the "object" of the ethical aim. The benefit from such an approach to ethical issues is based on the following:

a) that esteem for oneself does not result from the (a priori) realising of one's own selfhood (e.g. human dignity), but from the motion of reflection, in which the positive valuing of certain actions is carried over to their initiator;

b) that supplementing this motion of reflection by the "object" of the action – relating to another person (signifying the introduction of a dialogical sphere) – becomes necessary;

c) that recourse to just institutions becomes a supplement to this sphere (and an essential supplement, due to the fact that the "object" of the action may be an anonymous Other).

These are three fundamental and unavoidable components of the ethical aim, i.e. achieving the (a) good life, (b) together with and for another person, (c) in just institutions.[7]

Taking the theory of narrative into account leads to a broadening and hierarchizing of the concept of action, and further – to its raising to the level of *praxis* (action that has its goal within itself). This hierarchy is of significance for the ethical aim. It is generated by the concept of the "model of perfection" within each *praxis*, enabling assessment of actions pertaining to a given *praxis* (and moreover: to the creation of norms, the normalising of this *praxis* in terms of the degree of perfection). As a result one may speak of "immanent goods" within a given *praxis*. And this concept creates a foothold for reflexive (non-solipsistic) self-esteem and lending content to the categorical imperative. This then enables a connection of the teleological and deontological areas.

In addition the theory of narrative provides an opportunity for merging individual actions into comprehensive projects (life plans). The term "life" here signifies the person as a biological and cultural whole, at the same time

[6] Ibidem.

[7] Ibidem, p. 172.

surpassing the sum of the various *praxis* in which the person in question happens to be involved at a specific moment. A bond obviously exists between life plan (the *ergon* of man as man) and the models of perfecting each of the practices in which he is participating. As such one could talk of the residing within oneself of various purposes (of those immanent in relation to a given *praxis* and of a purpose merging various practices with an all-encompassing "plan of life"). This last dimension results from the frequent verification of our first life-path decisions, e.g. choice of occupation, the decision to become a parent, choosing to be a political activist, etc., verification not considered by Aristotle, but taken into account for example by Jean-Paul Sartre.

Life here means the biological grounding and unity of the whole of man, who casts an embedding look over himself (suffice here to cite the thought of Socrates, according to which unreflected life is pseudo-life). The concepts of good life, narrative unity of life, and life plan are synonymous but not identical (placing the emphasis on different aspects). All introduce a bond between *phrónesis* (practical wisdom) and *phrónimos* (oneself as practically prudent). The hermeneutic point of view makes a powerful mark here, as the constant effort of interpretation of action and of oneself as the one acting is linked to searching for conformity (harmony) between what seems best in regard to our life plan, and what governs the practices in which we participate.[8]

A type of hermeneutic circle appears here between the ethical aim and specific choices: the vision of the good life influences the most significant decisions regarding our existence (choice of career, emotional bonds, usage of free time, etc.), while these – subjected to reflection in their specific manifestation, influence in turn our vision of the good life (its retention or transformation). The whole influences the parts, and the parts – in reverse – the whole, just as happens in the interpretation of a text. This is connected to – or even conditioned by – the fact that the interpretation of the "text" (i.e. content) of an action is also the interpretation (i.e. understanding) of its doer: *"man is a self-interpreting animal,"* as Charles Taylor put it. Such self-interpretation in turn is the basis for esteem for oneself, which in turn brings an ethical point of view into play. This self-esteem shares the fate of interpretation: it provides the basis for a conflict of interpretations.

The question emerges, though, about the connection between the first element (aiming for the good life) and the second: "life with others and for others" (which Ricoeur describes as solicitude, though not to be mistaken for Heidegger's care). The French philosopher maintains that, contrary to the tendency to withdraw into oneself that characterises reflectiveness, solicitude

[8] Ibidem, p. 179.

cannot be conceived and experienced without respecting the Self; therefore its dialogical dimension, at first hidden, develops. According to Ricoeur this occurs as follows: the self is already worthy of esteem for its "I can" (and not only for having done), including for "I can" on an ethical plane (after all, I can assess myself and others ethically). This capacity of giving ethical judgments, declares Ricoeur, is in turn mediated by another. And this is because he believes that – contrary to the theory of natural law – man does not exist as a complete subject, i.e. equipped with his full range of subjective rights, before entering society. Therefore we do not have the grounds to expect from this society (or state, as its representative) protection totally independently of our readiness (i.e. internal commitment) to participate in tasks related to perfecting the social bond. And this signifies acknowledging the mediating role of the other.

Aristotle grasped this mediating role via the key role of friendship, which (1) does not belong to the realm of psychology but ethics, and which (2) is situated between the aim for the good life covered by reflection ("an ostensibly lonely virtue," according to the French hermeneutist) and justice (political virtue pertaining to a plurality of subjects). Friendship brings the issue of mutuality (reciprocity) into the foreground: a friend loves a friend not as his *alter ego*, but as the person he is (in his otherness not determined by being useful or pleasant "for me"). He sees in his friend the good-that-he-is, which does not eliminate reflexivity but sublimes it, splitting it through reciprocity.[9]

Due to its mutuality, friendship sits next to justice. They differ in the presence of institutions guaranteeing the realisation of proportional equality (since friendship assumes equality in rank). He-who-is-himself is guided towards another by a certain deficiency (i.e. a need). The friend, as an *héteros autos* (another self), takes on the role of the provider of what one is unable to have by oneself: the need for having friends derives from "[...] the very relation of the self to its own existence."[10] (One should add here that Aristotle did not introduce the concept of otherness, and as such Ricoeur adopts from him only reciprocity, sharing, and living together).

The initial reflexive moment of aiming for the good life is self-esteem. Friendship (without detracting anything) adds reciprocity to this in the relations between human beings, all of whom esteem themselves. Equality, as a consequence of this reciprocity, opens the way for the concept of justice. And therefore reflexiveness entails solicitude, which in turn entails justice.

In taking a critical approach to how Aristotle viewed the attributes of solicitude, Ricoeur wants to develop a uniting concept of solicitude based on

[9] Ibidem, pp. 182-183.

[10] Ibidem, p. 186.

an exchange between the (in principle equal) giving and receiving (on another note, this means a questioning of what he considered the one-sided ethics of Levinas). Ricoeur analyses this (fundamental) equality (i.e. mutuality), constituting an "fragile balance," from the angle of the phenomenon of "regard for others," grasped not in the aspect of obligation, but as "benevolent spontaneity", situated within the ethical aim.[11]

In order to show this spontaneity, Ricoeur analyses a situation the opposite to an instruction: the suffering of another. The initiative of sympathy is a spontaneous gift of he-who-is-himself. That it is not only pity is determined by the return gift of the sufferer: a reminder of the uncertainty of mortal fate (i.e. the shared conviction of human insignificance).[12] This spontaneity of the ethical reaction to another's suffering involves the constitutive participation of feelings (affects), which without a doubt are among our motivations.

Thus we have two extremes: 1) a summons/command, constituting an initiative from the other, in which the asymmetry is mitigated by recognition of his authority (in the sense of "being a master"); 2) sympathy for the sufferer, which is the initiative of he-who-is-himself, in which the initial asymmetry is removed as a result of the sharing with him of the conviction of mortality. And between these we have friendship, where equality (symmetry) is assumed, because he-who-is-himself and the other share alike the wish of living together.[13]

This searching for equality through inequality determines the position that solicitude has in ethics: the reverse influence on he-who-is-himself such that he begins to perceive himself as another among others. Ricoeur examines this new insight by breaking it down into three elements: (1) reversibility (of roles), (2) the nonsubstitutibility (of persons) and (3) similitude(of bonds), reaching the conclusion that "[...] I cannot myself have self-esteem unless I esteem others *as* myself."[14]

It is our French hermeneutist's belief that a sense of justice is already included in the very concept of the other. This leads him to posit two hypotheses (becoming theses during his research): (a) that the good life extends to cover the life (i.e. the functioning) of institutions (b) that justice displays ethical attributes that solicitude does not yet contain (for example the demand for equality). This in turn inclines him to distinguish the two most important elements for investigating the idea of justice: (a) of institutions as places for its realisation, and (b) of equality as ethical content of the sense of justice. Grasped together they lead to the defining of the self as anyone.

[11] Ibidem, p. 190.

[12] Ibidem, p. 191.

[13] Ibidem, p. 192.

[14] Ibidem, p. 193.

Ricoeur portrays the institution more from the perspective of a community of history, tradition and customs than its consequences – of coercing regulations of which it is the upholder. In order to show the precedence of the will for living together over legal and political systems regulating this will, he refers to the distinction introduced by Hannah Arendt between power in common and domination. The former is more primeval than the latter, as it derives directly from the category of action (pertaining to human plurality), which cannot be reduced to the category of labour or the category of work. "Plurality" and "action in concert" are constitutive for it. "The plurality includes third parties who will never be faces,"[15] claims Ricoeur, thereby explicitly overstepping the metaphysical circle of ethics in the style of Levinas.

This inclusion of the third calls for institutionalisation; without it, it would be something momentary, and not lasting. Power as an expression of the will for acting together and living together establishes for the ethical perspective a base thanks to which justice may enter as the third dimension of ethicality.[16] John Rawls' concept admittedly shows that the idea of justice may be embraced in terms of deontological ethics ("morality" according to the terminology adopted by Ricoeur), performing against the tradition of teleological ethics embodied by utilitarianism. But Ricoeur believes that by rejecting this last concept one can make use of the findings of Aristotelean ethics, because what is just pertains on the one hand to what is legal (the legal system), and on the other – to what is good, although at the same time overstepping interpersonal relationships.

Ricoeur rightly observes that the sense of justice (he prefers talking of it thus than of an "idea of justice"), though most often accomplished in the creation of legal regulations, is not exhausted in them. This can be seen for example in the fact that we are more sensitive not towards justice but towards injustice (which stubbornly occurs despite the existence of laws). Justice, understood as "to each what they deserve" leads (already with Aristotle) to the idea of distribution (of goods and burdens). Ricoeur proposes that the term "distribution" (i.e. apportionment) be understood broadly and flexibly, as containing an element (aspect) of distinction that is lacking in the concept of the will for acting together. This is because a distinction of shares is important: the equality that distributive justice thus understood is about is not arithmetical, but depends on the relation of "giving" to "receiving a share."

The concept of distribution ensures a "transition from the interpersonal level to the societal level within the ethical aim."[17] It allows for going beyond both sociologism (after all society is something more than the sum of its

[15] Ibidem, p. 195.

[16] Ibidem, p. 197.

[17] Ibidem, p. 200.

members) and methodological individualism (which reduces sociology to a science defining the similarity of individual behaviours): the institution as a system of distribution (of roles) is something more than the factual sum of the individuals as bearers of these roles, although this does not mean the introduction of some kind of metaphysical social beings. The institution as a rule of distribution exists insomuch as individuals are participating in it.

Such an understanding of institutions brings down the wall between the individual and society, at the same time ensuring cohesion in the three elements of the ethical aim: individual, interpersonal and societal.[18] Equality is the core of distributive justice, while the synonym of injustice is inequality. Obviously this does not mean arithmetic equality independent of share (of contribution of work, position and merits, etc.). Thus Aristotle and Rawls toil rightly to find such a conception of equality that does not lead to egalitarianism.

Ricoeur in the meantime adds to this the assertion according to which equality means for existing institutions what solicitude means for the existence of interpersonal relations.[19] However, in opposing the empty cult of institutions expected "to sort everything out," the French hermeneutist declares that the sense of justice does not lessen solicitude since it presumes it. And this is because it is within it that the uniqueness of people appears. On the other hand, justice increases solicitude since humanity as a whole becomes the area of equality's application. Nevertheless, adds Ricoeur, the idea of distributive justice features a certain ambiguity: on the one hand it refers to the idea of belonging, while on the other – to the idea of separation (i.e. no understanding for the interests of others when realising one's share/contribution and executing one's reward).

Kant's formalistic ethics, though it broke – in its intention – with teleological (and eudaimonistic) tradition, remains tied to it by a certain thread. Because this tradition also seems to indicate formalism as a valuable supplement, since one can discover hidden anticipations of universalism (characteristic of the deontological-formalistic perspective) in the teleological perspective.[20] With Aristotle, for example, this is the establishing of *mesotes* (the middle term, the intermediate) as a common criterion for all virtues (moral strengths). The same universality applies to the "in-each-case-mineness" of being-oneself in Heidegger's *Sein und Zeit*.

On the other hand, Kant's deontological conception seems to be connected to teleological aspirations: the moral obligation is tied here to the aim for the "good life." This is emphatically shown by the central position that the

[18] Ibidem, p. 201.

[19] Ibidem, p. 202.

[20] Ibidem, p. 204.

concept of good will takes in Kant's conception (e.g. in his *Groundwork of the Metaphysics of Morals*), as well as by the command he articulates in his second grasp of the categorical imperative, for always treating a person also as an end and never only as a means. In addition – observes Ricoeur – the approach according to which will becomes the bearer of the meaning of "the good" retains its continuity with the ethical perspective deriving from selfhood, since the confirmation of such a concept of will can be found in the capacity (of him guided by rationales) of establishing the beginning "among the course of things." And it is this capacity – as we already know – that is in Ricoeur's opinion the source (or also the subject) of self-esteem.

"The will, however," observes the French hermeneutist, "takes the place in Kantian morality that rational desire occupied in Aristotelian ethics."[21] The rationality of desire was recognised from the subject and the direction of its aspiration, while the rationality of will – by its attitude towards law. This difference can also be seen at a lingual (semantic) level: will is expressed in imperatives, while desires are "speech acts in the *optative* mode."[22]

According to Ricoeur four elements constitute the foundation of the deontological theory of morality developed by Kant:

a) good will as a description of the good without restrictions;

b) the criterion of universalisation (applying to the maxim of action);

c) (moral) legislation based on form itself (in keeping with the assertion that morality exists, "assuming that the sheer legislative form of the maxims were by itself the sufficient determination basis of a will")[23];

d) autonomy (recognising the connection between the concept of good will and the concept of action performed out of obligation).

In the Kantian understanding, establishing oneself as the (ethical) legislator does not lead to an egological thesis (i.e. the precedence of I over We or They): Kant positions his theory beyond the alternative of monologicality and dialogicality. As he moves from unity via plurality towards "everythingness" in his successive formulations of the categorical imperative, he uses only categories of quantity from his categorical table. But "unity" is not the "unity of the isolated ego," but the unity of "the universality of will" grasped before its splitting into a plurality of people.

Guided by this categorical apparatus, Kant develops his categorical imperative from form (expressed in the formula: "Act only in accordance with that...") via matter (expressed in the formula: "[...] humanity, as much in your

[21] Ibidem, p. 206.

[22] Ibidem.

[23] I. Kant, *The Critique of Practical Reason*, transl. P. McPherson Rudisill, posted 2012, http://kantwesley.com/Kant/CritiqueOfPracticalReason.pdf, p. 34.

own person as in the person of every other...," emphasising the meaning of the person as an end in itself), up to the realm of ends (constituting the complete definition of all maxims). In referring to Kant's deliberations regarding the sources of evil – for example his *Essay on radical evil* from *Religion Within the Bounds of Sheer Reason*, in which he asserts, among other things, that "evil is radical [...] as a natural proclivity, it cannot be eradicated through human power"[24] – Ricoeur develops his own version of the categorical imperative. This goes as follows: "Actsolely in accordance with the maxim by which you can wish at the same time that what *ought not to be*, namely evil, will indeed *not exist*."[25] This sentence combines both types of ethics, showing simultaneously the necessity of assimilating oneself via the teleological ethics (an aspiration for the good as the aim for the good life)of the sciences to which we owe deontological ethics(the theory of morality in the style of Kant). Because evil has come to exist in the world, our aim for the "good life" must – claims Ricoeur – put itself to the test of moral obligation.[26]

In his next step the French hermeneutist seeks a bond linking solicitude, i.e. the dialogical structure of the ethical aim, with a norm – and specifically with the norm of respect owed to people. Once again he refers to Kant, looking for a solution in the motives that inclined him to supplement the general wording of the categorical imperative with the reference to the concept of the person. Ricoeur sees the formula of the transition between solicitude and Kant's "second imperative" in the so-called Golden Rule, i.e. the principle of reciprocity. This, as we know, has two forms: negative, worded by Hillel, a Jewish teacher of St Paul, and positive, formulated among others in the Gospel according to Matthew (22: 39). The recommendation given in the negative formula is: "Do not do unto your neighbor what you would not hate him to do to you,"[27] while the positive one of St Matthew is: "Love your neighbour as yourself." These formulae are not entirely equivalent: Hillel's is better at balancing the norm of reciprocity, and it is this particular norm that governs ethical conduct, even if in categorical commands of the type "You shall not kill" the bond that these interdictions have with the Golden Rule is veiled.

The symmetricity of the Golden Rule – as Ricoeur rightly observes – opposes the dissymmetry of the protagonists of ethical action, which places one in the causative position, and the other in the position of one experiencing the action, and as such potentially in the relation of torturer and victim. As

---

[24] I. Kant, *Religion Within the Bounds of Sheer Reason*, transl. P. McPherson Rudisill, posted 2013, http://kantwesley.com/Kant/RationalReligion.pdf, p. 61.

[25] P. Ricoeur, *Oneself...*, op. cit., p. 218.

[26] Ibidem.

[27] Ibidem, p. 219.

if responding to the accusations of all those who – like Foucault, Habermas or Derrida – accuse hermeneutic thought of focusing on the aspect of sense and its assimilation while at the same time avoiding the aspect of rule and power, Ricoeur states that: "The occasion of violence, not to mention the turn toward violence, resides in the *power* exerted *over* one will by another will. It is difficult to imagine situations of interaction in which one individual does not exert a power over another by the very fact of acting."[28]

"Power-over" is the opportunity of the evil that violence is. The latter may be portrayed in the most general manner as a lessening or total destruction of the "capacity-to-do" of others.The form of interdiction that is beginning to dominate in morality ("You shall not steal," "You shall not falsely accuse," etc.) derives from the morality's resolute "No!" in response to the evil that violence of this kind constitutes. But, in Ricoeur's opinion, this does not lead to recognition of the (deontic) primacy of morality over (teleological) ethics. Because affirmation is original: solicitude as the mutual "exchange of self-esteems," and constituting the "hidden soul of prohibition."[29] It is this, he says, that "arms our indignation" when it is rejected.

In his next step Ricoeur presents an argument in favour of the thesis that the "respect owed to persons" expressed in the second wording of the categorical imperative remains in morality in the same relation to autonomy as, on the ethical plane, solicitude is to "the aim of the good life." The second formula, in his interpretation, becomes "the seat of a tension between the two key terms: that of humanity and that of the person as an end in himself or herself."[30] The idea of humanity here constitutes a supplement to the "abstract universality that governs the principle of autonomy, without the consideration of persons. The idea of persons as ends in themselves, however, demands that one take into account the plurality of persons [...]."[31] However, it does not go so far that one would be able to derive from it the essential otherness of other people, i.e. the idea of otherness. Continuity guaranteed by the idea of humanity collides (in a hidden manner) with the non-continuity introduced by the dissimilarity of people (as ends in themselves). Ricoeur even claims that the concept of humanity removes the otherness lying at the foundations of the diversity of people. He also refers with some scepticism to the Golden Rule, raising its insufficiently formal character (manifested in the introduction of elements from the sphere of inclinations: of what is pleasant or unpleasant for somebody). In defining Kant's thought in greater detail, Ricoeur states

[28] Ibidem, p. 220.
[29] Ibidem, p. 221.
[30] Ibidem, p. 222.
[31] Ibidem.

that "the rule of reciprocity lacks a discriminatory criterion that would allow a decision to be made in the thick of these affections [love and hatred, sympathy and aversion – A.P.], establishing a distinction between a demand that is legitimate and one that is not."[32]

Ricoeur does not agree with such a formalistic elimination of the emotional sphere from ethicality, and also strives to demonstrate that one can interpret the second wording of the categorical imperative as formalisation of the Golden Rule. Both these two rules have the same aspiration – to establish reciprocity where its absence has emerged, for example as a result of the non-symmetricity of force (i.e. the capacity to act) between one acting and one experiencing action, an absence frequently leading to violence (the emergent superiority being taken advantage of).

As one should expect, Ricoeur then expands his investigations into the ethical-moral sphere in relation to "the individual's care for himself" (the expression of which is the basic wording of the categorical imperative) and solicitude for a specific other (which reflects the second formula of the categorical imperative) – thereby achieving the effect of fullness – into the ethical dimension of anonymous interpersonal relationships, in which solicitude is replaced by justice. "It is to institutions, we said, that the virtue of justice is first applied."[33] Therefore he moves on to research into the conditions for the existence of just institutions as structures constituting the effect of the will for living together, ensuring lastingness, cohesion and identity for human communities. At the same time he admits that Rawls' theory contains the best contemporary conceptualisation of the idea of justice; this relates in its formalism to Kant, but differs from it in its rejection of the transcendental foundations.

Ricoeur makes a thorough analysis of the assumptions and consequences of Rawls' theory – unfortunately there is no room here for presenting and assessing this analysis – reaching the conclusion that the antiteleological character of his deductions is also valid in relation to utilitarian ethics, but not for Aristotelean ethics, the ethics of the good life. In his opinion, one can show that the idea of what is *just* "looks" in two directions: towards the "good," and – as an extension of solicitude to cover "everybody" – towards the "legal": "to such a degree does the prestige of justice appear to dissolve into that of positive law."[34] This second aspect is quite obvious: law established by a community should be a reflection of the idea of justice prevailing in the said community.

---

32 Ibidem, p. 223.
33 Ibidem, p. 227.
34 Ibidem, p. 228.

The first theme is interesting: the connection of the idea of justice with the aim that the good life is in a well-organised society.

According to Ricoeur, a certain pre-understanding of what "justice" and "injustice" means lies at the foundations of Rawls' theory of justice as "fairness" and the social contract as a constitutive "founding fiction." "This practical pre-understanding," says Ricoeur, "is the exact parallel to the attestation of the fact of reason [such as is freedom, which in turn conditions the existence of morality – A.P.] on the dialogic plane of practical reason."[35] The deontological theory of justice (i.e. its procedural grasp) does not manage to break the connection with the human feeling of justice that precedes this theory and accompanies it at all times.

The particular type of synthesis of the teleological and deontological understandings of ethics, represented so brilliantly by Aristotle's and Kant's ethics, a synthesis described by Ricoeur as a dialectic, must lead to the question regarding Hegel's place. The author of *The Phenomenology of Spirit* "sublated" – in the meaning of this term characteristic of his philosophy (*Aufhebung*, i.e. removing while retaining what is of value) – Kant's ethics, renewing the substantialistic, materially filled ethics in the spirit of Aristotle. However, he raised it above the position of an individual's good life to the level of the spirit, meaning to the historical state of human development as a society organised in some manner (a nation). Ricoeur is aware that his own depiction *implicite* in vokes Hegel. *Explicite*, though, it rejects the ethical proposition based on the concept of ethicality (*Sittlichkeit*, decency), which would fulfil the role of the third instance, capable of reconciling the claims of the ethics of the good life and the ethics of moral obligation. What inclines him towards this is the lesson that analysis of the phenomenon of tragicality gives to ethical reflection. As opposed to Hegel's conception of tragicality in the ethical aspect, Ricoeur states that:

> Tragedy [...] is not to be sought only at the dawn of ethical life but, on the contrary, at the advanced stage of morality, in the conflicts that arise along the path leading from the rule to moral judgment in situation. This path is non-Hegelian in the sense that it takes the risk of depriving itself of the resources of a philosophy of Geist [the spirit – A.P.]. I have discussed above the reasons for this reticence. They have to do with the mistrust of Sittlichkeit, which a philosophy of Geist requires placing above morality, and with respect to his political philosophy – more specifically, to the theory of the state to which all these deliberations lead. My wager is that the dialectic of ethics and morality, in the sense defined in the preceding studies, develops and resolves itself in moral judgment in situation, without the addition, as a third agency, of Sittlichkeit, the flower of a philosophy of Geist in the practical dimension.[36]

---

[35] Ibidem, p. 239.

[36] Ibidem, p. 249.

In speaking out against the solution proposed by Hegel, Ricoeur declares that the source of ethical conflicts is not the one-sidedness of the characters, but the one-sidedness of the moral principles, unable to cope with the complexity of life. In a situation of ethical conflicts, which become unavoidable as a result, a recourse to the Hegelian *Sittlichkeit* does not help: what is essential is a *"recourse to the ethical ground against which morality stands out."*[37] In his opinion, such is the path to the ethical wisdom of judgment in situation.

However, this does not mean a total rejection of *Sittlichkeit*; it only ceases to fulfil the role of an instance superior to ethics and morality, becoming one of the "places in which practical wisdom is exercised."[38] Diverse institutions of social life (manifestations of the objective spirit according to Hegel) do not eliminate moral conflicts, which is why even the best political philosophy is unable to replace moral philosophy (putting this into Hegel's language, it means that *Sittlichkeit* cannot supplant/abolish *Moralität*). This becomes perfectly visible, says Ricoeur, in the idea of distributive justice, the ambiguous structure of which can already be seen at a lingual level in the distinguishing into share (in producing common good) and division (the good received in exchange). The impossibility of introducing obvious criteria here, ones acceptable to all participants in the distribution, unveils the possibility of conflict. The tension between the demand for justice and the demand for equality, fundamental to Aristotle's conception (and later adopted by Rawls), comes into play here. Conclusive procedures introduced by various theories of just distribution only react to something that emerges independently of them and exists despite them. The idea of legitimation related to law is in constant (potential) tension with the idea of justice that escapes precise formulation. In particular legal atomism, ignoring the existence of bonds between individuals, is becoming a challenge for the latter. In this context Ricoeur is inclined to acknowledge Hegel's merits related to criticism of civic society as a realm of interests competing with one another, and to supplement the concept of a civic society with a political society, which Ricoeur sees "as the sole recourse against fragmentation into isolated individuals."[39] This ties the political (institutional) with the ethical sphere, because since an individual "becomes human only under the condition of certain institutions," then the "obligation to serve these institutions is itself a condition for human agent to continue to develop."[40]

If, however, we were to grant the rule of justice a broader scope than anticipated by Hegel or Kant, and if we free the phenomenologically delight-

[37] Ibidem.

[38] Ibidem, p. 250.

[39] Ibidem, p. 254.

[40] Ibidem.

ful analyses of *Sittlichkeit* (ethicality *resp.* decency) from becoming embroiled in the Hegelian metaphysics of the Spirit, then the contradiction between *Sittlichkeit* and *Moralität* becomes superfluous, and even harmful – concludes Ricoeur after contemplation. There is no instance in the realm of ethics higher than individual moral awareness, but it is distinguished by its triple structure comprising (1) the principle of autonomy, forming this entire sphere, and the related (2) principle of respect for people and (3) the principle of justice. The searches within the spirit of the nation for an instance higher than this awareness foundered against historical experiences – which were not to be shared by Hegel, but which became part of the 20th century (nationalism, fascism and communism). In the case of the conflict between moral awareness and the spirit of the nation, Ricoeur's sympathy lies unequivocally on the side of the former. And as moral awareness cannot be reduced to the universalistic formula of a categorical imperative, then democracy respecting the uniqueness of the individuum (with his own form of moral awareness), as a system of wielding power in society, becomes in Ricoeur's eyes an ethically distinguished form of political power. He agrees with Claude Lefort, that "democracy is born out of a revolution at the heart of the most fundamental symbolism from which all the forms of society stem; it is the system that accepts its contradictions to the point of institutionalizing conflict."[41]

However, let us not venture into the realm of political philosophy, which is emerging so interestingly in the above deliberations of the French hermeneutist. To bring things to a close, let's return – by way of recapitulation – to strictly ethical issues. Ricoeur would not have deserved the title of one of the greatest thinkers of the 20th century if not for proposing innovative solutions in this field as well, boldly stepping beyond the canons. This refers not only to Hegel, whose philosophy of the (cult of the) state he rejects as ethically dangerous metaphysics, but also to Kant. In his interpretation of the Kantian philosophy of morality Ricoeur also proves himself a master of properly construed deconstruction: on the one hand he acknowledges that autonomy (self-legislation) is a meta-criterion of morality, while on the other he asserts that Kant's theory of ethicality has to be subjected to broad revision, which would overturn the order of consolidation by casting doubts on the primacy of the principle of autonomy in relation to the principle of respect towards the other as a person, and to the principle of justice that is constitutive for the plane of institutions.[42] Because he believes that the non-egological and non-monologic (and therefore pre-dialogical) status of the autonomous self

---

[41] Ibidem, p. 260.

[42] Ibidem, pp. 273-274.

(i.e. of he-who-is-himself) "can be saved only at the end of a regressive path starting from the idea of justice, crossing through the principle of respect owed to persons in their plurality and in their otherness, in order to reach *in fine* the principle that states in what way the category of the most disadvantaged has to be taken as the term of reference for all just distribution, and in what way the one who receives my action – its potential victim – has to be respected asan equal of the agent I am."[43]

In Ricoeur's opinion only such an approach opens the possibility of correctly grasping the tragedy of action, related to the necessity of retaining two frequently clashing "ethical orders": that based on the universalistic claim, and that citing values constituting an element of the historical and communal development of a given community. Practical wisdom as moral judgment in situation has the task of mediating between these two orders, and overcoming the antinomies that have resulted from them. This is only possible when we recognise that "an autonomy that is of a piece with the rule of justice and the rule of reciprocity can no longer be a self-sufficient autonomy."[44]

At one point Ricoeur dresses his deliberations on ethics, presented in a few chapters of the voluminous treatise *Oneself as Another*, in the description "little ethics."[45] In ending this naturally brief presentation of the French philosopher's subtle and extremely rich and, it would seem, productive arguments on ethical topics, let as attempt to grasp the key issues in the stance he has proposed in a few succinct points:

a) practical wisdom wishes to bring about a reconciliation between Aristotle's *phrónesis* and Hegel's *Sittlichkeit* via a reinterpretation of the moral philosophy of Kant, while retaining the primacy of ethics (the good life) over morality (obligation/duty);

b) this priority means that the starting point is "good-hearted" (unreflected) *phrónesis*, while the destination is "critical" *phrónesis*, which takes into account the fundamental moral commitment commanding that "there be not what there should not be, and namely evil";

c) this critical *phronesis*seems to be Hegel's ethicality (*Sittlichkeit*) reinterpreted such that the possibility of any absolute knowledge at all (i.e. victory of the Spirit over contradiction)is removed. *Sittlichkeit* thus amended is protection "against any temptation of [ethical] anomie" so visible in the totalitarian societies of the 20th century.

---

43 Ibidem, p. 274.

44 Ibidem, p. 275.

45 Cf. also P. Ricoeur, *Refleksja dokonana. Autobiografia intelektualna*, transl. P. Bobkowska-Nastarzewska, Wyd. Antyk, Kęty 2005, p. 50.

The hermeneutic character of Ricoeur's "little ethics" emphatically highlights two aspects: the first, tying his investigations with the Heideggerian hermeneutics of *Da-sein*, is the seeking of sources of ethicality in the aspiration of human individuals towards self-fulfilment (to being-oneself), the fullness or crowning of which – using Heidegger's terms – is determined by a readiness to listen to the voice of conscience,[46] the second, Gadamerian, is emphasis that the fundamental goal of hermeneutic philosophy is wisdom (and not originality: new, original theses or methods). This moment is caught brilliantly by Elżbieta Wolicka in her valuable analysis of Ricoeur's reception of Kant. This is how she puts it:

> Ricoeur's deliberations head towards the conclusion that the goal of the philosophy of action, and essentially of philosophical anthropology in general (in the perspective of hermeneutic philosophy this is a certain version of the traditional 'practical philosophy'), is achievement of the supreme dianoetic virtue, i.e. wisdom. In other to achieve this goal, one should not lose sight of the specific dialectic of ethical experience and the moral norm. Ethics, contemplation over a person's experience in action, and the theory of morality, reflection over the normative dimension of this experience, are consistently "forming alliances with each other," without losing sight of the different points of view of their investigations. The a priori principles of formal deontology deserve, perhaps, to be "covered by the dust of oblivion," but this does not mean an absolute elimination of the morality of obligation from the horizon of practical philosophy.[47]

The normative stance provides a valuable criterion for our self-appraisal (exposed to diverse illusions) and the correctness of our situational interpretations of the Golden Rule. Practical philosophy practiced in a hermeneutical spirit does not equip us with indisputable, a priori ethical principles. Its task is rather to exercise our ethical "sense of tact."[48]

---

[46] Interestingly, the matter of where this voice comes from is left unresolved by Ricoeur. Cf. ibidem, pp. 68-69.

[47] E. Wolicka, *Rozważania wokół Kanta. Prolegomena do filozofii kultury jako krytyki władz podmiotu*, Towarzystwo Naukowe KUL, Lublin 2002, p. 284.

[48] Ibidem, p. 285.

Chapter 6

An Interpretationist Ethics

In this chapter I would like to draw attention to the dearth of ethical deliberations in Polish philosophical debates of the current conception that interpretationism constitutes. Despite quite dynamic growth in this philosophical movement in Western Europe and in the USA, it does not have – as far as I am aware – any representatives in Poland, while Polish translations of the works by its leading representatives are very few and far between.[1] This is a substantial omission, because not only in my opinion does interpretationism deserve at least some attention, not to mention thorough research and studies. Despite being aware of the proximity of their philosophical stance to hermeneutics, the creators of interpretationism do not fully agree to being included under hermeneutic philosophy, even as broadly understood. As such, we shall begin our presentation of their ethical considerations with a brief introduction of the main theses and ideas of interpretationism. For this purpose I shall refer to the selected works of two main representatives of the philosophy of interpretation (as interpretationism is sometimes defined), and so Hans Lenk and Günter Abel.[2]

[1] One of the few exceptions is the translation of a collection of articles by Hans Lenk entitled *Filozofia pragmatycznego interpretacjonizmu*, which edited and translated by the invaluable Zbigniew Zwoliński was published in 1995 by the Warsaw – based Oficyna Wydawnicza (in the *Terminus* series).

[2] H. Lenk, born in 1935 in Berlin, is a retired professor of Karlsruhe University, author of an enormous number of publications which, if listed, would burst the seams of this footnote; Günter Abel, born in 1947, is Director of the Institute of Philosophy and History of Science at the Technical University in Berlin; he publishes primarily in the renowned Frankfurt-based Suhrkamp (I shall list his main works in a later footnote). Also sometimes included among the representatives of this direction are Josef Simon (whose *Philosophy of the Sign* has been published

As the author of these words, I have no doubt that interpretationism[3] is an effect of the hermeneutic turn in philosophy. One may quite boldly claim that it is one of the main forms of this turn, alongside hermeneutic philosophy in the *sens stricto.* It differs from hermeneutic philosophy particularly in the fact that it acknowledges not understanding but interpretation as the main philosophical category, which in turn leads to Nietzsche being considered the pioneer of this trend more than Schleiermacher or Dilthey. However, despite further significant differences in regard to hermeneutic philosophy, one cannot help but notice that the latter philosophical approach or direction has much in common with interpretationism. This affinity is valuable if only because of interpretationism seeking inspiration not only in classic German philosophy (where, apart from Nietzsche, Kant is also a central figure), but also in Anglo-Saxon philosophy – mainly analytical and pragmatistic. Suffice here to mention that Abel spent many a year in the USA, where he worked closely with such philosophers as Hilary Putnam, Nelson Goodman, John R. Searle and Dagfinn Føllesdal. Traces of his readings of the works by his analytical colleagues and teachers, but also the classics of this movement – such as John Austin, Gilbert Ryle or Wittgenstein – are pervasive in his own works. However, this does not signify a lack of originality, as there is no equivalent of the conception he formulates either in the USA or in Europe.

As we know, Nietzsche himself distanced himself *explicite* from hermeneutics. However, this applied to the hermeneutics of his day, interested mainly in the exegesis of difficult fragments of the Holy Scriptures and the creation of a certain theory of a kind of exegetic interpretation. The fact that he was to become the father of the philosophy of interpretation, so close to hermeneutics, is due to the role of the concept of interpretation in his philosophy of life.[4] "There are no moral facts, only moral interpretations of facts." Such

---

in Polish as *Filozofia znaku*) and Tilman Borsche (translations of his articles have appeared in *Kwartalnik Filozoficzny* and the collective work that I edited, *Język – Świat – Rozumienie*, Expol, Włocławek 2007).

[3] Interpretationism is also defined by the very originators of this direction – as mentioned above – as "the philosophy of interpretation." However, when applying this terms interchangeably one must bear in mind that this is not about an ordinary "theory of interpretation" that any philosophical conception may possess (as the elaboration of a certain aspect of experience – ofconsorting with sense-containing creations), but about a philosophy for which the concept of interpretation constitutes the fundamental category, organising the entire philosophical consideration over reality and rationality.

[4] I wrote of the significance of Nietzsche's writings for the development of hermeneutic philosophy in my book *Hermeneutyczny zwrot filozofii* [Hermeneutic Turn of Philosophy], Poznan 2005 (pp. 79-97) and in the paper "Nietzsche i hermeneutyka," in R. Kozłowski, K.C. Cern (eds), *O filozofii Fryderyka Nietzschego*, Wyd. Naukowe UAM, Poznan 2006, pp. 13-28)

statements not only placed the concept of interpretation in the centre of attention, but also unveiled the mediation of our being-in-the-world via the act of interpreting. We conceive something *as that and not something else* based on interpretational constructs, which we accept consciously or subconsciously, constructs in which there is always an element of preliminary knowledge of the world. Lenk, wishing to emphatically articulate this fundamental significance of interpretation, even says that the famous "In the beginning was the Word" from the Gospel of John could be understood as meaning: "In the beginning was interpretation." In elaborating on the significance of this phrase he refers not only to Nietzsche, but above all to Kant and to the late neo-Kantian, Cassirer.[5] The latter claimed that man is an *animal symbolicum*, that we live in a "symbolic universe." Lenk takes this to a higher level, declaring that man is "a 'meta-symbolising animal,' and so a being functioning via the agency of symbols and symbolisation, i.e. a being only capable of understanding itself via symbolic interpretation [...]."[6]

When describing the stance of his philosophical ally, Günter Abel, Lenk claims in turn that:

> [...] the Kantian conception of transcendental idealism, according to which we ourselves to some extent impose upon the world our own forms of perceiving and interpreting, and the Nietzschean version (in which there is an emphasis on the general momentousness of interpretations, only thanks to which we can reach the facts – since "facts as such do not exist, there are only interpretations" – and ascertain their dominant role in our grasp of the world) may be combined in interpretationism.[7]

In the text cited here one clearly sees that Lenk senses a certain slight difference between his own grasp of interpretationism and that written by Abel. This is in the greater or smaller radicalness (*resp.*cautiousness) in the choice of phrases, which can also be seen in how Lenk strives at all costs to show that the stance he proposes is a modern take of Kantianism, admitting so-called *a priori* historization, i.e. variability of the categorical apparatus, the effect of which is a base interpretation of the world, while Abel – radical in his phrases – relates more strongly to Nietzsche, to his theses on the infinite number of possible interpretations of reality, and his conviction that it is the will to power that is the real motor and subject of interpreting.[8]

---

[5] Cf. H. Lenk, *Filozofia pragmatycznego...*, op. cit., p. 20 et seq. In regard to the significance of Kant for the emergence of hermeneutic philosophy, see Chapter 1 of my book *Hermeneutyczny zwrot...*, op. cit.

[6] H. Lenk, *Filozofia pragmatycznego...*, op. cit., p. XXIII [transl. from the Polish – J. Weber].

[7] Ibidem, p. 14.

[8] I have written more on the topic of historization in the article "Historyzacja a priori – zdrada czy produktywna kontynuacja filozofii transcendentalnej Kanta," published in

Common to both philosophers is of course the fundamental conviction that reality is an interpretational construct, and a multidimensional (multi-level) one at that. "The highest fundamental principle of the philosophy of interpretational constructs therefore proclaims: Any cognition and action, any perceptible existence, is – if we get to know it, or if we (can) name it at all – an existence saturated with interpretations. [...] The world in the extent to which it is cognisable is, one could say, a world depending on our interpretations. We can interpret it with signs only, with systems of notions and symbols depending on interpretations, etc. We conceive the world of what can be grasped, the world of phenomena, in structures created (in advance), similarly as Kant saw it, but we do so in a more flexible manner.The boundaries of interpretation are the boundaries of the cognisable (*erfaßbare*) world."[9]

In Lenk's opinion Abel grasped the same in his "law of interpretation" (*Satz der Interpretation*), according to which "man may perceive and describe reality only within – or as an internal function of – a defined interpretation schema, which he himself (as a living organism organised in a particularly manner) is. [...] 'He interprets everything that exists: [...] There is no reality, there are only interpretations.'"[10] The final sentence shows at the same time a greater radicalness in the phrases of Abel, who substitutes Lenk's phrase "the limits of interpretation are the limits of the perceptible world" with the succinct "the limits of interpretation are the limits of the world." However, when taking a closer look at these phrases, then I would say that you can see that the difference between them is "diplomatic" in character: Lenk does not want to situate his conception as oppositional to realism, as he believes that a realistic interpretation of the world – at least in the sense of an elementary interpretation of material and biological reality – is essential not only for the meaningfulness of human practical (especially technical) but also theoretical (cognitive) actions. Even if this would only be so-called internal realism.

But I think that Abel would also agree with the assertion that reality that is external in relation to our consciousness does exist, although its form given to us is a product of our interpretational activity. Lenk in turn agrees with Abel's suggestion that elementary (primeval) interpretation is carried out as it were automatically, due to the facilities of the human organism and his will of survival. "The fundamental division of the phenomenal world," says Lenk,

K. Śnieżyński (ed.), *Immanuel Kant i świat współczesny. W 200. rocznicę śmierci Immanuela Kanta*, Wydawnictwo Wydziału Teologicznego UAM, Poznan 2004 (pp. 67-80).

[9] H. Lenk, *Filozofia pragmatycznego...*, op. cit., p. 29.

[10] Ibidem, p. 12. The quote within the citation is from Günter Abel's book *Nietzsche. Die Dynamik des Willen zur Macht und die ewige Wiederkehr* (Berlin – New York 1984, p. 184) [transl. from the Polish – J. Weber].

approvingly citing Gerhard Roth, "into three fields – namely the world around us, our body, and the world of our mind – is also a construct of our minds. The basis for this division is sensorimotor interaction with one's surroundings [...] The brain makes this division because it is of decisive importance for the body's survival."[11] And he provides an excellent example for the fact that for an organism endowed otherwise the reality would have to take on other colours: "Even the biologically programme dproto-interpretations can be imagined as fundamentally different: we could for example possess a magnetic sense which factually we do not possess."[12]

Abel's contribution to the theory of interpretationism is mainly a very detailed and analytical elaboration of what interpreting thus grasped involves, what its types are, what layers of reality are thus constituted, and what role in all of this is played by human nature (the biological organism, the senses) and what role by culture (language, knowledge, history). This enables the creation of an impressive theoretical construct which probably has no equal in contemporary philosophy, a construct that Abel presented in his three main works[13] and in a large number of well-known and cited articles. An attempt at delving into the details of this conception as part of this presentation would be unfeasible. Let us therefore bring our sketch up to a state that will allow us to: (1) present the ethical conception resulting from it, and (2) assess it, referring also to the political consequences of this ethical conception.

As living beings we are equipped with a mind, and "condemned" to interpreting what we encounter on our path – as claimed consistently by both Lenk and Abel. "We are incapable of not interpreting! *Interpretari necesse est, interpretatio indispensabilis.*"[14] Yet this does not mean that all our interpretations are products of our imagination or of our cognitive creativity. By analysing the human grasp of reality, Abel reached the conclusion that there are three types (or main types) of interpretation. One of these has the character of primeval interpretation, or proto-interpretation – and this applies to our grasps of the reality that is external in relation to our own, and is conditioned by our sensory apparatus. Unlike the others, this type of interpretation is in principle invariable. "In principle," because hypothetically we would be able to imagine that we are intelligent organisms equipped with a different sensorial apparatus, which would result in a different appearance of the reality-for-us. The fact that

[11] Ibidem, p. 45.

[12] Ibidem, p. 43.

[13] These are: *Interpretationswelten. Gegenwartsphilosophie jenseits vom Essentialismus und Relativismus* (1993), *Sprache, Zeichen, Interpretation* (1999) and *Zeichen der Wirklichkeit* (2004) – all published by Suhrkamp Verlag.

[14] H. Lenk, *Filozofia pragmatycznego...*, op. cit., p. 48.

only reality-for-us is accessible to us is, in the light of the accepted Kantian-Nietzschean (perspectivism!) assumptions, equally as obvious as the fact that we correctly conclude that this reality-for-us is an "appearance (view)" of the reality-in-itself that we don't experience, but that we logically assume. (Of course another possible interpretation is that reality is our individual figment and that it vanishes together with our death, but as a methodical construct this loses against the conviction that this elementary, empirical reality survives our death, and in this sense is objective.)

Due to the rank that the concept of interpretation has within hermeneutic philosophy, interpretationism wishes to distance itself from hermeneutics, as only by doing so can it perform as an independent philosophical conception. Certain subtle differences undoubtedly exist, especially when comparing Abel's and Gadamer's conceptions. The task of creating a distance in relation to hermeneutics is also facilitated by the latter being grasped only as "appropriative interpretation" (*aneignende Deutung*), which essentially is the interpretation-of-something-given (*Interpretation-von*): of a comment, a work of literature, a picture, or a sculpture. Yet for Abel something more primeval than this is *Interpretation-als*, i.e. interpretation of something as something, i.e. specifically that and not something else, e.g. a piece of painted canvas as a picture). He seems to forget, though, about the existence of that "hermeneutic-as" preceding the "as-apophantic" (i.e. a comment declaring something about something), as after all it constitutes the basis of Heidegger's hermeneutic turn in philosophy.[15] It would therefore seem that there is no impassable border between the interpretationism of Abel and Lenk and the hermeneutic philosophy elaborated in the spirit of late Dilthey and Heidegger from the middle period of his work. However, let us leave this theme aside so as not to complicate our reasoning unnecessarily, and return to the description of interpretationist philosophy.

One can – says the author of *Interpretationswelten* – distinguish three grades and three aspects of the concept of interpretation.

> As for the grades, then from the appropriative interpretations let us call them in brief "Interpretation 3" (for example of the processes of creating theories and hypotheses, explanations and justifications); one can distinguish unifying patterns (*Gleichförmigkeitsmuster*) that have become established within us, become something habitual through accustomization; let us call them in short "Interpretations 2." Conventions, as well as practices and competences acquired culturally and socially, belong here. From these two [types of interpretation – A.P.] one can distinguish components residing in the categorising and individualising functions of our usages of language and signs, named in short "Interpretations 1." Logic concepts such as "existence" and "subject" may be classified into this area, as also may the principles

[15] Cf. M. Heidegger, *Being and Time*, transl. J. Stambaugh, State University of New York Press, New York 1996. For more on the subject, cf. L. Bottani, "Przekaz, dialog i komunikacja. Martina Heideggera koncepcja języka," transl. E. Andrzejewska, in B. Andrzejewski (ed.), *Komunikacja – rozumienie – dialog*, Wydawnictwo Naukowe UAM Poznań 1990, pp. 21-26.

> of temporal-spatial localisation and individuation. These are always established in any given organisation of experience [...].[16]

Abel brings to the attention of those who might have difficulty speaking in reference to the last area of interpretations that the grasp of something like a chair, and of something different such as a feather, requires the acceptance (silent in most cases) of certain assumptions, assumptions that make interpretations out of these grasps. At the same time he declares that this area (or level) of interpretation is elementary, i.e. connected with the emergence of the sphere of objectivity and its accompanying issue of empirically ascertained authenticity. That it is not a product of the subjectively passive acceptance of reality's influence on man, but an actively creative interpretational relationship is shown by the fact that adopted categorising concepts may be questioned and replaced with others.[17]

Interpretationism's proximity to hermeneutic philosophy is also demonstrated by Abel acknowledging the meaningfulness of speaking of the "unity of the world," similarly to Gadamer, who talks of "one world and one reason," despite the multitude of cultural and historical worlds and the multitude of historical forms of human understanding. Abel distances himself *explicite* from the constructivism of his master and friend, Goodman.[18] (Also telling, in this context, is the sub-title of his main work on interpretational worlds: *Beyond essentialism and relativism*, entirely in keeping with the spirit of hermeneutic philosophy.) This does not mean, though, that the relationship between world and interpretation is the same at every rung of interpretation. If a scientific hypothesis belonging to area I3 does not help understand empirical reality, then we question it – this hypothesis – rather than that reality. But when there is a change in the horizon of understanding and practices related to I1 (the original categorisation of reality), then we are beginning to deal with a different world. Putting it briefly, says Abel, "on level I3 interpretations depend on what they interpret, on level I2 there is an allocation of interpretations and worlds, while on level I1 such-and-such-worlds depend on the interpretations, i.e. when adopting criteria of meaningfulness one cannot concoct, individuate or specify a world-in-itself, totally independent of the processes of interpretation."[19]

[16] G. Abel, *Sprache, Zeichen, Interpretation*, op. cit., p. 27 [transl. from the Polish – J. Weber].

[17] Although Abel does not write of this, I believe he would agree with the suggestion that a comparison of the categorisation of various cultures carried out, for example, by Ludwik Fleck, also confirms this aspect of the interpretationist conception.

[18] G. Abel, *Sprache, Zeichen, Interpretation*, op. cit., p. 31, footnote 7 (also: "Interpretationsphilosophie. Kommentare und Repliken," *Deutsche Zeitschrift für Philosophie* No. 44, 1996, pp. 903-916).

[19] Ibidem, pp. 31-32.

At the same time it is obvious that the life practice accompanying each of the interpretational levels is different. Which is why, claims Abel, one can talk about a three-fold sense of interpretational practice. First of all he has in mind the manner – shared with other members of one's lingual and action community – in which "syntactic, semantic and pragmatic features of lingual signs and non-lingual actions and experiences are determined and defined. Then it is about situating each human utterance, thought, capacity and knowledge in the area of non-lingual action, reaction and behaviour. And finally – about anchoring these two interconnected complexes in an elementary, source-type and unavoidable interpretational practice, being what Wittgenstein defined as that 'that must be accepted, that is given.'"[20] As we know, the Austrian philosopher believed that just knowing the meanings of words is insufficient for communicating. In his *Philosophical Investigations*, specifically in note no. 242, he expressed this in the form of an assertion: "If language is to be a means of communication there must be agreement not only in definitions but also (queer as this may sound) in judgments,"[21] which means: sharing a certain knowledge regarding reality.

The concept of life practice that "manages" interpretations shows that interpretationism is situated far from the fundamentalist philosophies seeking ultimate justification or incontrovertible certainty. The theory of Abel and Lenk is much closer to the philosophy of life, including in its latest manifestations (Ferdinand Fellmann, Hermann Schmitz), which can be seen, inter alia, in the meanings imparted to human corporality for the constituting of the world given in the interpretation. If Abel speaks of certainty, then he rather has in mind interpretative-practical certainty, which one does not look for, because one – by participating in a certain life practice – is already within it. Which is also why Abel adopts from Wittgenstein not only his understanding of certainty ("The reasonable man does *nothave* certain doubts," writes Wittgenstein[22]), but also and above all the criterion of externalism. Applied to lingual practice, it leads – as we know – to rejection of the possibility of a private, meaning an internal, language. Abel even goes further, and says that, in parallel to the above, one could also argue against the possibility of totally private action.[23] Naturally this last statement has consequences for the ethical conception he developed.

---

[20] Ibidem, p. 34.

[21] L. Wittgenstein, *Dociekania filozoficzne* [Philosophical Investigations], transl. B. Wolniewicz, Wydawnictwo Naukowe PWN, Warszawa 2000, p. 129.

[22] L. Wittgenstein, *O pewności* [On Certainty] (note 220), transl. M. and W. Sady, Spacja, Warszawa 1993, p. 53.

[23] G. Abel, *Sprache, Zeichen, Interpretation*, op. cit., p. 36.

Interpretationism is not a metaphysical stance that would render the ontic existence of reality dependent on the occurrence of interpretation. By no means does it claim that something such as facts does not exist, since only interpretations exist. Facts do exist, but they are interpretations (or the results of interpretation), which means a grasp of something external in categorial terms adopted beforehand, consciously or otherwise. Interpretationism is situated beyond the opposition of realism (empirical-physical) and idealism (e.g. mentalistic). It is a stance that applies to the sense and not the existence, and if existence, then understood as sense, meaning in the Kantian meaning of realness as belonging to the category of quality. The existence of interpretations does not mean for him insurmountable relativism, but only problems with communication in regard to reality. Yet these are problems that can be overcome, since the "will for communication overcomes relativism,"[24] while by word of explanation he adds: "Attention here focuses rather on what one can say something about sensibly in a critical approach, and about what one cannot. The subject here is always the subject [given – A. P.] in cognition or in interpretation."[25]

It is time to interrupt this necessarily brief description of interpretationism as a philosophical theory and move on to the related practical philosophy formulated *explicite* by Abel, or rather the germ of such a philosophy. In concluding this short presentation, we should also point out that, according to this conception, then – firstly – wherever we are dealing with the substantially (in terms of time and cause) ordered world of experience, acts of interpretation have already been established in which the empirical material is embraced in schemata and categories, and that – secondly – the forms of elementary interpretation and its horizon consolidate not only the possibility of talking about subjectivity, but also about authenticity.[26] It must be added here that alongside the three levels of interpretation Abel distinguishes three aspects of the concept of interpretation: the logical, the aesthetic and the ethical. Applied to our basic conceptual system (in the narrower sense), the components constitute an "interpretational logic." The forms of sensory view involved in the application and understanding of symbolic signs may be grasped collectively as "interpretational aesthetics," while the normative components of interpretational practice, as well as the regular and situation-appropriate usage of signs, as "interpretational ethics."[27] According to Abel, there is an internal connection between these three aspects of interpretation.

[24] Ibidem, p. 44.

[25] Ibidem, p. 46.

[26] Ibidem, p. 57.

[27] Ibidem, p. 30.

Contemplation of the ethical proposals of interpretationism is interesting in that the above description did not reveal any fundamental incompatibilities between this stance and hermeneutic philosophy. For example the salience of interpretation (instead of understanding) is not such, as neither is the diminishing – in my opinion unjustified – of hermeneutics' interests to a single level of interpretation (the interpreting of artefacts of spiritual culture). Interpretationism, deriving partly from the debates and problems that analytical philosophy had become embroiled in, naturally strives to use much more precise language than hermeneutic philosophy. But this does not alter the fact that they are very similar (related) conceptions, if only one acknowledges that hermeneutic philosophy ends neither with Heidegger nor Gadamer. Even the role of language, presented in interpretationism from the perspective of accepting the existence of many sign systems (that cannot be reduced to speech, i.e. to natural language) does not constitute here a barrier in communications between these two directions, as long as one steps beyond Gadamer's position towards Heidegger's contemplations on language contained in *Being and Time.*[28] What differentiates hermeneutic philosophy and interpretationism the most is the latter's underestimation (not signifying depreciation) of the role of tradition, which also covers pre-existing reason. This leads to a desire to construct our reference to reality as if from scratch. We shall see if this also means the same in the ethics proposed by interpretationism. Because this diagnosis by hermeneutic philosophy – a correct one in my firm opinion – cannot be entirely avoided.

Ethics, and especially philosophical ethics, is characteristic knowledge, and namely is knowledge serving action. Let us begin therefore from the interpretationist grasp of the relations between knowledge and action. Abel proclaims that these areas belong to each other, while at the same time questioning any reductionism by which knowledge is reduced to something that is solely in the service of action, or by which action is reduced to the role of the producer of knowledge. According to this Berlin philosopher one can already see this mutual irreducibility in the fact that languages suitable for describing these two fields must be different. "Knowledge and action [...] are human activities that flow from the world of life and are fulfilled within it."[29] Therefore any attempt at achieving a philosophical grasp that unites them while at the same time retaining their separateness must mean the creation of a certain philosophy (theory) regarding the "world of life" (*Lebenswelt*). Worlds of life are obviously not something that is supra- or pre-interpretational: they are worlds given in

[28] Cf. on this matter: J. Liptow, "Zur Rolle der Sprache in Sein und Zeit," in B. Merker (ed.), *Verstehen nach Heidegger und Brandom*, Meiner Verlag, Hamburg 2009, pp. 27-46.

[29] Ibidem, p. 300 [transl. from the Polish – J. Weber].

interpretation. The philosophical theory of worlds of life should therefore be created within the boundaries of the general philosophy of interpretation. A philosopher of interpretation reveals aspects of actions based on analysis of knowledge and aspects of knowledge based on analysis of action, "because one cannot be [...] conceived without the other."[30]

The ethical implications of interpretationism

The thesis regarding man's fundamentally interpretational reference to reality (both in the aspect of its cognition and in influence on it) has a number of consequences for interpretationist ethics. The first and perhaps the most important of these is the rejection of the possibility of the existence of a One and Only Metaphysically Established Rightfulness or an Exclusive and Irrefutable Truth. In terms of ethics, this negatively expressed circumstance is very significant, as it undermines the possibility of the philosophical sanctioning of any metaphysical, epistemological and religious fundamentalisms (and fanaticisms). That there is no position that somebody could take to achieve privileged access to the truth signifies a turn in the direction taken by such normativeness that is internal in character, a turn related to the constituting of signs and their interpretations without external borrowing and references to something transcendental. Such ethics is characterised by the fact that it "leaves other people their different signs and interpretations, and me – my signs and interpretations, and my nterpretations of other signs and interpretations."[31]

The first feature of interpretational ethics is its tolerance for the rules and ways of living of other people, other nations and other cultures. To emphasise this, Abel uses the term *Anerkennung*, recognition, popularised by Hegel. However, he distinguishes the broader meaning of this term, signifying a certain type of transcendental (in the sense of contra-factual, pre-empirical) assumption, which every one of us does when functioning within a certain communicational community. Recognising the signs and the rules for their interpretation in force in such communities is essential for one to function rationally (effectively). Such recognition takes place automatically, via the very participation itself. As human beings, says Abel, we are always in mutual sign-and-interpretation relations with other people. Secondly, one cannot be

[30] Ibidem, s. 303.

[31] G. Abel, *Zeichen- und Interpretationsethik*, p. 2. (Quoted according to page numbering of the manuscript sent to me, and which will be a chapter in the book I am editing, *Ethik im Lichte der Hermeneutik*. This book was published by the Würzburg publisher Königshausen & Neumann) [transl. from the Polish – J. Weber].

somebody individual without relating to others, without acknowledging them. "Taking things logically, when I ask: 'Why should I acknowledge other persons at all?,' then these other people are already in play."[32]

The process of personal individualisation is only possible in relation to the previously acknowledged otherness of other people. However, such acknowledgement is not the same as the ethical concept of recognition, i.e. acceptance. Differentiating between these two notions is essential for three reasons:

1) The implicit inclusion in the relations of recognition of signs, norms or values functioning within a given community does not signify their explicit recognition, in the sense of conscious consent for everything that is in force.

2) Without this one cannot understand the possibility of a judgment addressing others that claims their activity to be unethical.

3) The possibility of ethical reflection, and therefore the question regarding the limits of recognition, also requires this differentiation.

Interpretational ethics, the foundations of which have been built by Abel, is situated beyond the dichotomy of ultimate justification *versus* relativism. It sticks with the necessity for rational justification (of actions, norms, principles), casting aside the metaphysical fantasies regarding final justification. It is – he says – an ethics "on a human scale," conscious of human finiteness. Which is why one speaks here rather of a "pragmatically final" justification, although this may always be subject to reinterpretation, a deepening, or rejection. In Abel's opinion such an ethics, based on human finiteness, does not signify acceptance of relativism or even particularism. That in turn is possible thanks to a peculiar inter-engaging of the (Kantian) elements of reflectiveness, ethical consideration and (Hegel's) elements of decency (*Sittlichkeit*, experienced ethicality).

In the contemporary world – claims the author of *Interpretationswelten* – we are not dealing with a scarcity but rather a surplus of norms and values, *ergo* with situations of them coming into conflict. This means that our being-in--the-world is saturated with normative-axiological elements. Abel even questions the sense of distinguishing between ethical actions (relating to values) and axiologically neutral targeted-rational actions (i.e. purely instrumental). In every instrumental action, ethical attitudes constitute the defining factor.[33] Making this distinction only obscures reality, condemning us to the unnecessary searching for a passage from axiologically neutral (purely instrumental) actions to ethically characterised actions. The very fact that human action is directed (condemned as it were) towards cooperation, coordination and communication makes it action that is moral in character. In this context Abel speaks of

[32] Ibidem, p. 3.

[33] Ibidem, p. 7.

the "public and internally-normative character of human actions."[34] Man does not enter the realm of morality; he is always within it. However, the surfeit of norms gives rise to disruption that one has to know how to eliminate without succumbing to fictitious amoralism. The main task for practical philosophy is to draw up procedures that could help in this.In reference to the deliberations of Rawls, Goodman and Føllesdal, Abel calls such conduct "the procedure of counterbalancing," and acknowledges it as a variation of the rule of "reflected equilibrium."[35]

In referring to Kant, our Berlin philosopher observes that neither action subordinated to some alien will nor action deriving from the self-interestedness of the person undertaking the said action constitutes ethical action. The ethical character of a particular action is determined by conduct in keeping with a precept (command) that we established for ourselves as rational beings. However, concluding the Abel is only referring to Kant's categorical imperative here would be premature. When he talks of the continuity taking place between justification based on the categorical imperative and that deriving from the normative structures of the world of life (*Lebensweltu*), he is clearly taking into account the rational norms and ethical practices already existing in the given community of communication.What is more, he gives them a kind of pragmatic priority. One could say that he combines Hegel's *Sittlichkeit* with Kant's *Moralität.*

When we function smoothly in society, the "normativeness of the *Lebenswelt* experienced" is enough for us. But there are situations in our lives when we have to ask the way. This is occurring for example in relation to the dynamic development in the biological sciences, generating ethical problems for which there is no automatic solution of the "world of life" in normativeness. For such cases the introduction of a procedure modelled on the categorical imperative is essential. However, Abel considers Habermas's interpretation of this – according to which it is the "intersubjective rule of universalisation" – as mistaken. In Abel's opinion, the categorical imperative is a "critical gauge for our ever-subjective maxims of actions and interpretations, pertaining to the question regarding whether the latter could function as principles of universal legislation."[36] In his opinion there is no possibility of carrying out such verification in the sphere of intersubjectivity.

The normal situation is then set out by life in keeping with the "experienced normativeness of the world of life." The moment when ethical reflection kicks in, in the form of the categorical imperative, occurs only when there are

[34] Ibidem, p. 10.
[35] Ibidem, p. 11.
[36] Ibidem, p. 12.

disturbances in this normativeness. Because of this, Abel talks of the complementariness of these two keystones of ethicality, with a certain advantage for "experienced ethicality." The ethicality of the world of our life does not yet result from the categorical imperative itself, as an ethical law generated by pure practical reason. This is why Kant himself adds to this the "uninhibited adoption of another's will for one's maxim," described by him with the term "love."[37] Only such recognition of an other's right to self-defined ethicality leads to the generating of a factually existing moral substantiality, elevating social life.

Although Abel prefers to refer to Husserl's notion of *Lebenswelt* and Wittgenstein's "forms of life" (*Lebensformen*) than to Hegel's *Sittlichkeit* (decency, most often translated into Polish as "ethicality"), there is no doubt that he accepts Hegel's amendment to Kant's ethics, as long as the rational core of the Kantian postulates drawing from an analysis of what is pure practical reason is retained. Using the terminology of Wittgenstein (form of life) or Heidegger (being-in-the-world, world-picture, etc.) would seem to be the result of a desire for communication with the reader undisturbed by "metaphysical" (speculative) elements. Of much greater importance is that he opposes the currently increasingly importunate parcelling out of ethics into specialised vocational ethics. "Concrete problems with the application of ethical principles," he writes, "are without a doubt today more complex, far-reaching and richer in their repercussions than they once were. Yet this is still about the application of ethics (for example in the field of medicine), and not about generically different regional ethics; as such it is rather about specific differences in the area of application, and not about general differences in the actual form of the ethics."[38]

In the light of the assumptions adopted by Abel, the answer to the question about why his ethics is anti-fundamentalist and anti-metaphysical is relatively clear. However, it is a little more difficult to argue on their basis against relativism, especially if it is understood as self-interestedness, characterising all cultures in a certain sense, and simple cultures to a high degree. Abel himself equates *Lebenswelt* with the world of culture. The only tool he has left to undermine the inviolability (sometimes ethically difficult to accept) of ethical norms regarding worlds of life alien to us – for example the custom of the genital cutting of girls in Islamic Africa, or the marrying off of 13-year-old girls in the Roma community – is discursiveness or reflectiveness, i.e. referring to the procedure of the categorical imperative. This demonstrates why Abel emphasises the whole time the "complementariness of the world-of-life and discursive justification," and together with this the standing of the "critical verification of moral trans-subjectivity."[39]

[37] Ibidem, p. 14

[38] Ibidem, p. 15.

[39] Ibidem, p. 22.

"The world of life, public character and discursiveness," claims this Berlin interpretationist, "in their internal relationship, then come across as pragmatically the last entanglement of the limitation, definition and justification of semantic and pragmatic attributes and the correctness of action, speech and thought."[40] Interpretationist ethics, focusing on the principle of equilibrium grasped reflectively (between my horizon/perspective and somebody else's perspective, and between the horizon of the individual and the community) and basing on the experienced normativeness of the *Lebenswelt* (but in a situation of disturbances referring to critical ethical reflection in the spirit of the categorical imperative), gives not only good foundations for both the new, hermeneutical ethics of responsibility but also for intercultural ethics. And there is no need to emphasise that in the globalising world of ethics these are taking on a particularly momentous significance.

In addition it is situated beyond the dichotomy of cognitivist ethics and non-cognitivist ethics.It is, as Abel puts it, an "internal ethics cut to human scale" (*interne Ethik nach Menschenmass*).[41] The reflective procedures he proposes do not dominate or tyrannise life, they do not place all actions before the tribunal of (ethical) reason. They only enter when necessary, carrying out the essential harmonisation. This is because the model that Abel uses is the model of untroubled understanding and also communication, the smooth functioning of which is only to be restored (and not constituted) by ethical consideration. This is also why in his ethics the Berlin philosopher uses the tripartite structure of interpretation: actions refer (for the purpose of justification) to maxims, while they refer to principles, and the footing for the latter is a certain vision of the world. "It is here that the spade meets the hard rock," says Abel, relating to Wittgenstein's well-known phrase. Why? "Because that is how we live, and not otherwise."[42]

This way of thinking is also reflected in another section of practical philosophy elaborated by Abel, and namely in the philosophy of politics. Although it has not yet achieved a developed form with Abel, one can discern its leitmotif: the idea of democracy. Why, asks Abel, is this particular form of wielding power superior to others? Is the majority to decidebecause – as the biblical Pilate believes – we do not know what truth is? Is relativism therefore the logical assumption behind the idea of democracy? And perhaps the most important question: Is it possible to justify the idea of democracy, to lend it credibility and rationality, while steering clear of the pitfalls of metaphysical absolutism on the one hand, and relativism replete with resignation on the

[40] Ibidem.

[41] Ibidem.

[42] G. Abel, *Sprache, Zeichen, Interpretation*, op. cit., p. 352 (Abel refers here to note no. 217 in L. Wittgenstein's *Philosophical Investigations*).

other? Abel answers this question in the affirmative, adding that such possibilities are afforded precisely by hermeneutic thinking, and specifically by interpretationist philosophy.[43]

One can already see its superiority at the outset: political order is recognised not as an element of the order of truth, but of the order of suppositions and convictions. Interpretationism differs from both the theory of discourse (Habermas/Apel), and from postmodernism (Rorty/Vattimo). Human life practice is, for him, originally marked not by discursiveness but by interpretationality. "Without interpretation [there is – A.P.] no communication and no practice."[44] This means at the same time that the normative components present in interpretative life practice acts of speech and action on every occasion. Ethical-political assertions are more deeply rooted in life than purely theoretical statements: not only is a verbal answer an indicator of their comprehension; so too is answer through deed, meaning the action that follows them. This, says our Berlin philosopher, is because conflicts regarding the issue of ethicality in politics are conducted with less distance and much greater emotional and existential involvement. However, let us return to our deliberations regarding democracy.[45]

There has been mention already of Abel rejecting both the dogmatism of the "ultimate justification" and the relativism of "anything goes." He portrays the sphere of life practice not from the angle of *episteme,* but from that of *doxa* (convictions). He introduces the idea of recognition (*Anerkennung*), carefully distinguishing the two fundamental ways of understanding it: basal, indicating that we – not being a priori in the possession of truth – are as it were forced to recognise, at least preliminary (for testing), the stance of another person, and the dissimilar factual recognition (approbation) of somebody's deeds or views. "Acknowledging the interpretational horizons of other people in their otherness and distinctness, implied by the philosophy of interpretation in the ethical aspect, derives internally from the very idea of interpretational relations. We are embroiled internally and not externally in issues of recognition. Referring to other people also remains a logical assumption of the fact that we do not want to acknowledge others."[46] This is because other interpretations by other interpreters are, and the whole time remain, admissible. But our consent for them is contingent.

---

[43] Ibidem, p. 341.

[44] Ibidem, p. 342.

[45] Due to lack of space I must omit Abel's interesting critique of the conceptions of Habermas/Apel and Rorty/Vattimo. It deserves a work of its own.

[46] Ibidem, p. 349.

In the language of political philosophy this means an initial situation of freedom and equality, although this is not synonymous with simple egalitarianism. Because the equality in question here is fundamental, it is transcendental (Abel prefers the phrase *sinnlogische Gleichheit*, hard to convey in Polish or English), drawn from the relations of interpretation, and not factual. In factual life practice inequalities are unavoidable, but as they lack metaphysical justification they are fluid. Abel believes that interpretationist ethics constitutes an important contribution towards lending greater credibility to the idea of democracy and making it rationally acceptable. Among other things, he shows how one can resolve the problem of the mutual relations of the two main values of democracy, equality and freedom. This does not mean that interpretationism wants to give further philosophical consolidation for democracy; instead of this Abel speaks of "taking responsibility for democracy."

"Democracy," says the author of *Interpretationswelten*, "is not an 'essentialistic and proper' solution of the issue regarding the form of political power, and in this sense it cannot be consolidated, supported on some kind of foundation. The strength of the idea of democracy lies in the fact that it does not have to embody any essentialism of the form of political power or lead to the relativism of discretion."[47] In order to clarify this, Abel indicates the fundamental difference occurring between relativism (devoid of any measurement, and *ergo* unexplicated) and the relationism given together with the adopted interpretational practice. "The former would lead to a discretion which, in factual speech, thought and action, is not actually there. The latter in turn is unavoidable in the fact that speech, thought and action entirely independent of the horizons of regularity and interpretation cannot exist in a critical aspect."[48]

These are the reasons why our Berlin philosopher is opposed to Rorty's phrase proclaiming the "superiority of democracy over philosophy." In his opinion it is a consequence of the silent adoption of a dichotomy: ultimate justification – the relativism of discretion and rejection of the idea of great narratives. In the meantime, says Abel, "democracy's precedence before philosophy would have to be replaced by another relationship of precedence: the precedence of fundamentally open and unending interpretational relations over defined and ever-limited interpretations."[49] There is no need to defend democracy from philosophy, as long as philosophy is understood as a theory of interpretational practices delimiting human being-in-the-world.

In this aspect postmodernism, of which Rorty is a leading representative, commits two mistakes: (1) in spite of itself, it absolutizes its stance as the

[47] Ibidem, pp. 351 and 362.

[48] Ibidem, p. 372.

[49] Ibidem, p. 371.

only possible point of view; (2) it does not notice the factual regularities and normativeness existing in any communicational community. After all, without constituting an ultimate justification, they are a point of support, albeit one that in critical reflection may be revised and reformed. This also explains why the idea of democracy is a consequence not of relativism, of an "empirically-relativistic worldview," but fundamentally of the interpretational relationism, characterising our life practice. And it is this that lends the ethos of democracy the character of something rationally acceptable, *ergo* something comprehending. Democracy does not result from deficit, but is the form of system that "best reflects the interpretational character of public acts of life."[50] One of the consequences here is that interpretations not acknowledged by the majority at a particular moment may acquire their recognition in the future. This is because these decisions are not based on absolute, unchallengeable objective knowledge, but have a "binding character at a certain moment in time."[51]

An extreme form of such a democratically taken decision is the abolition or suspension of democracy itself. The fact that this is possible was demonstrated to the fullest by the emergence of the Third Reich. Abel of course recognises such an eventuality. However, he adds that one may criticise it on three levels of argumentation: (a) theoretical, (b) practical and (c) legal-institutional. In his opinion the assertion that self-destruction is a logical consequence of democracy is itself a logical error, since such a conclusion is logically dependent on what it questions and abolishes."Therefore this conclusion, and not the assumption enabling it, democracy of freedom, is self-contradictory. Because it needs what itabolishes [...]."[52] On a practical plane, one can argue against the self-abolishing democracy using the Kantian idea of freedom as autonomy. "The right of the order of freedom, the right not to abolish oneself, is the sole right according to which I can respect that order without violating my own freedom."[53] This does not mean a limitation but an increase in positive freedom. On the other hand the abolition of democracy leads to an enormous limitation of such freedom.

The time is now right for a few sentences of recapitulating commentary. The reader familiarised with the developed forms of hermeneutic philosophy probably feel the need to reflect over the issue of the relations between interpretationism and hermeneutics. We must leave a more substantial consideration of this issue for another occasion, as it cannot be tackled within but a few sentences. We shall restrict ourselves here to stating solely that the difference

[50] Ibidem, p. 374.

[51] Ibidem.

[52] Ibidem, p. 369.

[53] Ibidem.

between Abel's and Gadamer's portrayals is much smaller than claimed by Abel himself. Nevertheless, this is not to say that such a difference – stepping beyond the choice of language for the narrative, which is much more precise with Abel – does not exist. What lies close to the heart of both philosophers is – on the one hand – a rejection of metaphysics, and, on the other, opposing discretion, associated with postmodernist relativism. Despite differences in their choice of narrative – with Gadamer relating to Hegel's social substantialism, and Abel keener on using the ethical formalism of Kant – the two philosophers are linked by an acknowledgement of the world of life, together with its internal sagacity (rationality), as a kind of ultimate point of reference. The fact that Abel opposes its absolutisation and conservation, and *ergo* potential conservatism (traditionalism), while Gadamer emphasises the role of tradition in our understanding of reality, is important but not decisive. After all Gadamer also fully accepts the necessity of social changes. Just like Abel, though, he is opposed to the omnipotence and violence of Habermas's ethics of discourse, attempting unrealistically to place everything that exists and functions before the "tribunal of reason" or "intersubjective consent." Therefore one can also see these stances' similarities in their reactions to the ideas of so-called transcendental hermeneutics, formulated by Habermas and Abel.

The fundamental similarity, revealing at the same time philosophical acuteness and the depth of interpretationism, can be seen in the rejection of both the idea of morality as a game, one in which "we can play, but don't have to at all," as well as of the alleged necessity put forward by the ethics of discourse of arguing in favour of the fact that "it is worth being ethical." Our life practice, claim Gadamer and Abel in harmony, is permeated by normativeness, a part of which constitutes normativeness of an ethical nature. We do not choose such a form of existence, but are, so to say, thrown into it. The claim that the understanding-interpretational rooting of human existence privileges democracy as a political system is *explicite* repudiated only by Abel, which does not mean that *implicite* Gadamer also spoke out against his master, Heidegger.[54] I believe the author of *Truth and Method* would agree with the majority of assertions made by the author of *Interpretationswelten.*

[54] In order to confirm this intuition, it is sufficient to study the three volumes of talks with Gadamer, the conversations conducted and edited after Heidegger's death by Carsten Dutt, Riccardo Dottori and Silvio Vietta. Particularly instructive in this respect is the book Hans-Georg Gadamer, *A Century of Philosophy: A Conversation with Riccardo Dottori*, Bloomsbury Academic, London 2006.

Chapter 7

A Hermeneutical Ethics: Prolegomena

Following the presentation (by necessity selective but striving not to miss too much of significance for the issue tackled in this book) of deliberations regarding the phenomenon of morality among the classics of a direction of philosophy currently termed hermeneutic philosophy, a few words of summary and comment are now due. However, both summary and commentary will step outside of the "source material" presented so far, as our goal will be to make ourselves aware of both the opportunities and limitations of an ethics constructed on the theoretical basis that hermeneutics constitutes. These deliberations are of a preliminary character, as there is nothing in the literature on the subject that could serve as a model or guiding theme, and as such we understand them as a prolegomena to the future hermeneutical ethics. We shall also take into account research embraced in works that, for various reasons, we have not considered to date. These include three books *explicite* exploring the issue that we are tackling here. I have in mind two books by the Dresden Philosopher Bernhard Irrgang: *Practical Ethics from the Hermeneutic Perspective* and *Hermeneutical Ethics. Pragmatical-ethical Orientation in Technological Societies,* and Gerhard Pfafferott's book *Ethics and Hermeneutics.*[1] However, none of these is the "hermeneutical ethics" we are looking for, fully consistent with the conception of Hermeneutic Philosophy that I have been developing over the last few years.

---

[1] B. Irrgang, *Praktische Ethik aus hermeneutischer Sicht*, F. Schöningh Verlag, Paderborn 1998; idem, *Hermeneutische Ethik. Pragmatisch-ethische Orientierung in technologischen Gesellschaften*, Wissenschaftliche Buchgesellschaft, Darmstadt 2007; G. Pfafferott, *Ethik und Hermeneutik. Mensch und Moral im Gefüge der Lebensform,* Forum Academicum, Bonn 1981.

Strength or weakness of philosophical ethics

In the conclusion to his first work, Bernhard Irrgang advises those hermeneutists tackling ethical issues to practice the art of modesty. After all there are things more important than ethics, he says, aware of the fragility of the place that ethics, and with it the entire practical philosophy, occupies in the lives of contemporary, liberal or even permissive societies. The basis of an ethics practised from a hermeneutic point of view is – as if Gianni Vattimo said it – an awareness of the end of the great narratives, and with them the limit to the undisputed reign of some sort of "fundamental principles," without which it was once impossible to imagine human coexistence. Nobody expressed this as emphatically as Odo Marquard in his celebrated essay *Farewell to Matters of Principle.*[2] At this point, almost incidentally to the main theme of our contemplations, it would be right to observe that this philosopher from Giessen was the first to show that the very emergence of hermeneutics was an ethically positive act, as it created the theoretical basis for overcoming conflicts deriving from diverse interpretations of the Holy Bible. We have an excellent analysis of the ethical standing of hermeneutic philosophy in Marquard's well-known paper entitled *The Question, To What Question Is Hermeneutics the Answer?*[3]

Vattimo's contemplations take a direction similar to Marquard's – although in relation to the hermeneutics of our day. Afraid that a hermeneutical ethics may fall into "the already overcome metaphysics," he too restricts it to the role of an instance supporting the attitude of openness towards dissimilarity, tolerance, respect, a readiness for dialogue, and an opposition to wrongdoing, etc. Although Vattimo refers to Gadamer, this is not to his ethical deliberations that we analysed in a previous chapter, but to his general hermeneutic theory, a thesis of which is that nobody can claim the rights to the final interpretation. The hermeneutic stance is in itself, in his opinion, of an ethically positive character. Vattimo's ethics, as Michał Januszkiewicz put it so elegantly, "is not an ethics of imperatives, but an ethics of goods that have arisen inside man."[4] Nevertheless, this does not seem to be all that one can say about ethics from a hermeneutical point of view. As a result of his unjustified worry of "falling

---

[2] O. Marquard, *Farewell to Matters of Principle: Philosophical Studies*, Oxford University Press 1989, pp. 3-21.

[3] Ibidem, pp. 111-140.

[4] M. Januszkiewicz, "Etyczny wymiar hermeneutyki (wokół Gianni Vattimo)," in A.F. Kola, A. Szahaj (ed.), *Filozofia i etyka interpretacji*, Universitas, Cracow 2007, p. 303. Similar and in my opinion excessive ethical minimalism is seen in Rorty's thinking. Cf. R. Rorty, "Etyka zasad a etyka wrażliwości," transl. D. Arbiszewska, *Teksty Drugie* 2002, no. 1-2, pp. 51-63.

into metaphysics," the Italian postmodernist – just like Marquard – does not step beyond truisms easy for all to accept.

Without questioning the ethical dimension of the very existence of hermeneutics, and accepting that concern itself regarding the dependability of an interpretation that does not impose its point of view, and does not want to appropriate what it interprets but allows itself to say something new (it wants, as one would say, to "surrender to the truth of the text"), is*par excellance*an ethical accomplishment, referring to the value that justice constitutes; worth emphasising is that our research intention goes beyond this dimension of the relationship between ethics and hermeneutics. It is something obvious to us. Hans-Martin Schönherr-Mann reflects this well in the *Introduction* to the book*Hermeneutics as an Ethics* when he writes:

> A certain ethical claim flows from understanding in an essential manner. [...] Being fair towards a thing, understanding it properly, i.e. not contemplating it solely from one's own perspective, not being guided purely by one's own interests, combines at the source hermeneutics and description with an ethical claim to justice.[5]

In our opinion, a hermeneutical ethics can actually be about something more than just concern for a "better understanding," even if this were to be a better understanding of what is ethical, e.g. other people's behaviours or motivations. Neither does the rightful observation that hermeneutics expands upon ethical thought by revealing an insight into the limits of ethics itself,[6] exhaust the ethical possibilities of hermeneutic philosophy. To realise this it is enough to refer to the works by Ricoeur that we have analysed, to his "little ethics," which compared to the fainthearted proposals of Rorty or Vattimo comes across as an "ethical giant," while not losing any of its hermeneutic moderation.

However, is – one should boldly ask – the assertion regarding the weakness of an ethics based on hermeneutic philosophy true? Has ethics, or rather has ethical inspiration lost all power of motivating human action? Or perhaps it never really had it, constituting but a useful ideology, a "false awareness," veiling the true state of things? Yet such a claim would be not only premature or risky; it is quite simply untrue.Worldview convictions, largely defined by an ethical component, were the motor behind the majority of the most significant events in human history, events both positive, generating new constellations of values, and events negative, signifying catastrophes of humankind. This is

[5] H.-M. Schönherr-Mann, "Hermeneutik als Antwort auf die Krise der Ethik," in H.-M. Schönherr-Mann (ed.), *Hermeneutik als Ethik,* W. Fink Verlag, München 2004, pp. 24-25. This work is a selection of essays on ethics written by representatives of hermeneutic and interpretationist philosophy [transl. from the Polish – J. Weber].

[6] Ibidem, p. 29.

rightly pointed out by Rolf Zimmermann, who in his book with the much-telling title of *Moral as Power*, writes:

> The power of morality is unveiled both in the good and in the bad. Because even events that we condemn morally derive from moral motives. Such a lesson may be drawn from those epochal catastrophes that arouse the greatest outrage. Yet after all the people responsible for the said catastrophes rely on the same kind of understanding of themselves, which cannot be adequately expressed in notions of "immorality" or "amorality." Here we are rather dealing with the phenomena of moral being-other or moral violation of boundaries, showing in a shocking manner that in history there are deep-reaching conflicts between diverse moral self-understandings. The question regarding the historical place of our own morality is resolved via the contrast to the kind of morality that we reject.[7]

This is why, for a complete grasp of the essence of the phenomenon of morality, it is certainly worth – alongside the phenomenological insights into the essence of moral experiences and analytical studies into the structure of ethical judgments and mind-sets, and alongside analysis of ethical systems, those already functioning socially and those designed by the great thinkers, by the spiritual leaders of humankind – making an attempt to understand epochal historical events as ethical experiences affecting mankind. One could, like Zimmermann, describe this as the "phenomenology of historical experience." In this definition Hermeneutic Philosophy sees a confirmation of the rightness of its path, leading after all from Husserl's phenomenology of "experienced life" and via Heidegger's "thrownness" to Gadamer's "effective history" (*Wirkungsgeschichte*) – an accumulation of historically elaborated initial knowledge (Gadamer's "tradition"), enabling for man an understanding participation in the existing reality, including in its ethical aspect. "The prospect is thus revealed for also grasping universalistic morality as a power joining the conflict of diverse moralities, in order to therefore argue in favour of its acceptance, its self-consolidation, and the broadening of its influence in as rational a manner as possible. From my perspective this means a hermeneutic reference to the language of human rights, understood as the language of historical experience, which in the meantime has become embedded in documents significant for the history of this world. The oft-posed problem of justifying the universality of human rights does not refer to a one, sole rationale, but to justification based on experiences that liberate entire motivational strata."[8]

---

[7] R. Zimmermann, *Moral als Macht. Eine Philosophie der historischen Erfahrung*, Rowohlt Verlag, Reinbek bei Hamburg 2008, p. 7. It would seem that hermeneutic philosophy could endorse such (and only such) a grasp of "human rights" [transl. from the Polish – J. Weber].

[8] Ibidem, p. 15.

A hermeneutic reckoning with Nietzsche

Nietzsche's thinking constitutes an enormous challenge not only for grasping ethics from a hermeneutic perspective, but also for a such-conceived "phenomenology of historical experience." The declaration that "God is dead" may be understood as an iconoclastic attack on religion, and in particular Christianity and Judaism. However, one can also, or perhaps even should, see within it an articulation of a phenomenon discerned by many in the 19th century, but which was only expressed quite so suggestively by Nietzsche. This phenomenon was a consequence – as Hegel would probably say – of the development of awareness of freedom, and thereby man's existential responsibility for himself in the face of the cold universe, indifferent to his fate. The topic itself, the "death of God," also contemplated as a speculative possibility by Hegel (in his treatise *Glauben und Wissen*), signified not only criticism of the institution of the church and the priesthood exercising institutional supervision over morality or criticism of the Victorian morality of the society in which the author of *Twilight of the Idols* had come to live. This criticism was intended above all as a liberating realisation of the existential character of humankind's being in the world, existential – meaning deriving from, if using Heidegger's terminology, thrownness, projecting and falling. However, the radical Nietzschean critique of the hitherto morality did not by any means signify a rejection of morality as such. Quite the opposite: it was actually Nietzsche who declared that nothing was more important than the great moral issues.[9] But this meant a continuation of the work begun by the Enlightenment, a "destruction of the old tablets," radically calling upon man to take responsibility for himself. We have to acknowledge this philosophically weighty accomplishment, even if we question the new "moral tablets" proposed by Nietzsche himself, and based on a cult of strength, health, vitality and creativity.[10]

The Nietzschean diagnosis remains in tune with the views of numerous thinkers of the 19th century, who due to the successes of the natural sciences leading to a dominance of their methodology, combined with the enlightenment cult of experience and the 'counting mind' (intellect), noticed the growing devaluation of religious convictions and their progressing subjectivisation (privatisation), which was accompanied by the secularisation of social life. We have already spoken in this context of Hegel, but should also mention

[9] Cf. F. Nietzsche, *Werke. Kritische Gesamtausgabe*, vol. 14, eds G. Colli, M. Montinari, De Gruyter, München 1980, p. 263.

[10] For the ethical consequences of Nietzsche's nihilism, compare Hans-Martin Schönherr-Mann, *Friedrich Nietzsche*, W. Fink Verlag, Paderborn 2008.

Karl Marx, Heinrich Heine and Max Weber, with his "disenchantment of the world." "God is dead" is a statement of the cessation of the validity of the absolute moral instance, which leads to the acknowledgement that it is man – his interpretation of existence – that creates values, and therefore also the revaluing of values.

At first this meant a deep crisis, since a new morality – liberated from the guardianship of tradition – seems to be an issue of an arbitrary creation of principles, norms and values, the validity of which – deprived of absolute sanction – seems to hang by a thread. But does this mean that "everybody has the kind of morality that they feel like"? Perhaps Nietzsche would agree with such an ascertainment, particularly if we were to apply it to the spiritual elite of humankind (a race of lords or Übermensch) and link it to his declarations regarding the will of power, which after all has different degrees of tension in different individuals, reflected in their different degrees of creativity, and *ergo* innate freedom – not guaranteed on the strength of personal existence or a social contract. We, however, taking a different path in his genealogy of morality, understood as critical reflection over the sources and functions of morality, relying in so doing on analysis of the historical experience, by no means have to agree to such a consequence. Especially – as Nietzsche says himself – that the individual is a product of our times, while the group – or as the author of *Thus Spoke Zarathustra* says, the "herd," is more primal.[11] Morality is a social phenomenon that can be generated by creative individuals – such as the Buddha, Socrates or Jesus of Nazareth – yet the form of his validity depends on whether there is, whether there exists a group that wants to recognise it as its own, i.e. desiring to live in accordance with it. Therefore a "private morality" is something equally as preposterous as a "private language" according to Wittgenstein.

One has to concede that Nietzsche is right when proclaiming the inadequacy of religious ethics in regard to the era in which he lived. Christian morality, he says, is a command, and its source is transcendental; it is therefore positioned outside of any possibility of discussion or critique. Its dominion depends on authentic faith in God, while its loss signifies a crisis of this morality.[12] The consequences of the situation outlined by Nietzsche are, on the

---

[11] *Thus Spoke Zarathustra* contains his exceptionally interesting observation: "Older is the pleasure in the herd than the pleasure in the ego: and as long as the good conscience is for the herd, the bad conscience only says: ego." This means that the herd (*Herde*) is older than the "ego," which emerged relatively recently. It is the herd (the group) that "determines" the voice of conscience. Cf. F. Nietzsche, *Thus Spoke Zarathustra*, ed. B. Chapko, feedbooks, 1(15) *The Thousand and One Goals*, p. 52 et al.

[12] Cf. F. Nietzsche, *Twilight of the Idols*, KGA VI, p. 114.

one hand, a weakening influence of religious ethics, and a growing requirement for a philosophical ethics, the philosophical equivalent of religious ethics, on the other. This is undoubtedly a crisis situation, of which the sole way out – and only achievable in the distant future – is the drawing up in the dialogue of humankind's spiritual leaders, political, religious and philosophical, of a certain minimum universal ethics applying to every person, and to humankind as a whole, an ethics that all those interested could subscribe to.[13] The situation of morality following the Nietzschean verdict signifies a pluralism of ethical projects, constituting a reaction to the loss of the "absolute institution" (at least as far as Europe is concerned), which leads to rivalry and even conflicts between them. The majority of these projects derive from the anti-Nietzschean idea of the possibility of creating a universal ethics appropriate for humanity in the future, even if they agree with the author of *On the Genealogy of Morality* in regard to the mundane (and not otherworldly) character of the phenomena of morality and ethicality.

Certainly Nietzsche cannot be considered the legislator or originator of such an ethics. His assertion, hermeneutic in spirit, that moral facts do not exist, but only a moral interpretation of facts, unveils the interpretational character of morality, making it an ally in the attempt at securing a more adequate grasp of the specificity of this phenomenon. The phenomenology of ethical historical experience, inspired by the Nietzschean "genealogy of morality," commands us to accept that the vision of man, of his place and task, contained in diverse moral systems – not only philosophical and not only religious (and constituting certain worldviews) – may constitute an enormous force, and sometimes, unfortunately, also a destructive force. The attempts at "creating new man" that we have dealt with in fascism, in national socialism, or in bolshevism (communism), were not based on a total rejection of all morality.[14] They were but a negation of the morality to date, morality that had arisen on a Christian tradition, and their replacement by a certain new morality. And as we know, these "tablets of new values" sometimes allowed for the performance – with a clear conscience – of deeds that, in the preceding ethical systems, would have been considered serious violations of the moral order and even crimes.

A hermeneutic ethical reflection, if only due to the importance of the concept of historically-effective consciousness (*wirkungsgeschichtliches Bewußtsein*), must carefully analyse not only the ethical projects created by the classics of

---

[13] At attempt at formulating the foundations of such an ethics is made by Rolf Zimmermann in the book cited above, *Moral als Macht...*

[14] An interesting analysis of these attempts is contained in the book by Gottfried Küenzlen, *Der Neue Mensch. Eine Untersuchung zur säkularen Religionsgeschichte der Moderne*, Suhrkamp, Frankfurt am Main 1997.

European philosophy, but also (and perhaps even above all) monitor historical experiences related to morality, and in particular projects inspired by visions of a new, reborn man, leading to historical catastrophes usually resulting from their fundamentalism and self-interestedness, from slavery or the Inquisition to the October Revolution, fascism and national socialism. For the hermeneutic approach it is obvious that the ethics expressed in the Convention on Human Rights, drawn up and enacted following the last of the above catastrophes of mankind, is not the result of discovery of some kind of absolute point of view, put a proposal deriving from European spirituality and the experience of European culture as well as cultures inspired by Europe (e.g. both the Americas). The awareness that it is not suprahistorical, but determined by history and historically embedded, does not have to hold Europeans back from propagating it as the basis for a universal ethics. On the other hand, neither does it provide the grounds for an unentitled sense of pride or looking with a sense of superiority upon all those unwilling to acknowledge its "obvious validity."

The fact that hermeneutic ethics relates to some degree to Nietzsche does not mean that it sympathises with the material aspects of his ethical project, such as the cult of force and the stronger, the rejection of the ideal of loving thy neighbour and feeling compassion for others, or a negation of altruism, equality, veracity and aspiring for the truth. An in-depth analysis shows the pitfalls of the Nietzschean critique of these values.[15] Moreover, in many aspects of Nietzsche's "revaluation of all values" the hermeneutical ethics is forced to notice aspects leading its followers or imitators close to anti-universalistic and even totalitarian thinking. It was no accident that such "racial imperialisms" – if one may use Florian Znaniecki's term – as fascism, national socialism or Zionism – cited Nietzsche's philosophy. As such it would be right to agree with Irrgang's claim that Nietzsche's moral theory, taken as a whole, is not fit for the role of the foundation of an ethics practised in a hermeneutical spirit.[16] Besides, the same applies also to Kant's moral philosophy. The valuable insights of these two philosophers, carefully distilled from their diverse writings, are certainly useful, though. What is interesting is that their analysis could bring about a revision of the meaning of their views as an entirety, an example of which comprises studies regarding the supressed assumptions of the categorical imperative and the logical cohesion of their diverse articulations.[17]

[15] Scheler gives an example of such critique, showing that Nietzsche did not understand at all what the Christian command for love was about.

[16] Cf. B. Irrgang, *Praktische Ethik...*, op. cit., p. 74.

[17] In his book on morality as a strength, R. Zimmermann indicates for example the "rule of [unity] of mankind," which is an assumption for the validity of the categorical imperative, and which Kant does not explicitly formulate anywhere (*Moral als Macht...*, op. cit., p. 100).

Religious ethics and philosophical ethics

The "death of God" understood metaphorically is the first phenomenon that we have to take into account if hermeneutic philosophy is to retain its claims for truthfulness, i.e. for universal, intersubjective validity – meaning a validity not only for the Euro-Atlantic circle of thought. Because even if we agree with the claim that transferring motivations deriving from religion to the private sphere, motivations characterising contemporary (western-) European spirituality, leads to a loss in the significance of the metanarratives that once generated enormous conflicts between people, groups or nations, then after all Europe cannot – if only due to globalisation, and thus growing mobility and its result of migration processes – be torn out of its international context. Besides, there is no doubt as to the strength of religion, together with ethics as its indispensable component, in the world outside of Europe. And Europe, not that long ago believing in the end of history, i.e. prevalence of the order of modernity it had developed, must accept this.

An ethics that is religiously motivated, and so derived from one of the Great Narratives, is not leaving and has no intention of leaving the arena of history, despite the crisis. This was rightly anticipated by Gadamer, reaching the conclusion that the most important task for philosophy as hermeneutics, and *ergo* philosophy of the future, would be to bring about a dialogue between the great religions with the purpose of enabling a peaceful and empathy-filled coexistence of mankind, especially in the face of the destructive possibilities afforded by contemporary military technology.[18] This task is tackled by hermeneutics based on its insights into historicity – *ergo*contingentness – of human being-in-the-world and in its interpretational character, derived from the fact that man (as rightly ascertained many years ago by Cassirer) is a symbolic being (an *animal symbolicum*). Hermeneutics, as Marquard observed in turn, grew from the experience of religious wars, and through its diagnoses made a significant contribution to their quelling, and as such it can share these experiences with the whole of mankind in order to prevent similar catastrophes in the future.

Hermeneutic Philosophy in itself therefore already contains an ethical component. This cannot be disregarded, although neither would I like to overrate it as Vattimo does, discerning a *panaceum* to the ethical dilemmas of this world in nihilism, which – in his opinion – is the legacy of hermeneutics broadened to take Nietzsche's thinking into account. The "weakening of ex-

[18] Cf. H.-G. Gadamer, *A Century of Philosophy: Hans Georg Gadamer in Conversation with Riccardo Dottori*, Bloomsbury Academic, London 2006.

istence" and "weak (i.e. anti-metaphysical) thinking" that he proposes could definitely contribute to a mitigation of fields of possible conflict.[19] However, they do not hand us the tools making it possible to cope with the problems we may face today (and problems we really are facing, if only in genetic engineering). What is needed here is a somewhat more developed and concretised ethics, even if there can be no explicit ethical theory derived through deduction from some universally accepted "first principles." In order to achieve this, the hermeneutical ethics must strive to become a philosophical ethics, aware of the pluses and minuses of such self-determination.

Despite no philosophical ethics possessing unambiguity or the motivational power characterising religious ethics, the horrors of the two world wars as well as diverse totalitarianisms and terrorism show that Nietzsche's thesis that "God is dead" (and with this a limitation of the effectiveness of religious ethics) is not entirely groundless, even if it does apply to different societies – and not only those outside of Europe – to different degrees. This in turn means that teaching ethics at school – by conveying the historically developed *ethos* of a given national community – constitutes a major need in the 21st century. Besides, this does not only have to occur via the inclusion of ethics in the school curriculum, although that would certainly be a step in the right direction. Important here is literature, a medium conveying ethical content, as indicated by Rorty and Ricoeur (and also, *implicite*, Gadamer, in his conception of the educational role of the classic works of literature that he called "eminent"), as too are the teachings of history. Hermeneutical ethics, which links the quality of the life of society directly with the strength and vitality (or, put simply, the quality) of traditions, emphasises – with a force incomparable to any other conception – the significance of moulding and education (*Bildung*) as the fundamental condition for the continuity and growth of culture, and its creative adaptation, while retaining what is most expressive and valuable, and what was developed by the generations preceding us. Which is why Rorty is right when he claims that the new generations will not learn the ethicality of coexistence from an analysis of the never-ending conflicts between experts in ethics, who break down the phenomenon of morality into details understandable only to those in the know, but from discussion led by somebody experienced in ethics and regarding contemporary problems related to decisions that have to be made affecting us and the world around us; in a world in which the first principles have given way to the principle saying that everything surrounding us is an effect of our understanding, our interpretation, which is never final.

[19] See G. Vattimo, *The End of Modernity*, Johns Hopkins University Press, 1991, and *Le avventure della differenza*, Garzanti Editore, Milano 1980.

What premises must a hermeneutical ethics start with? Naturally premises that derive from insights, from diagnoses in which hermeneutic philosophy has been involved in the almost two hundred years of its growth. These include the claim that reality comes across to us as bearing sense, as structured in some way, ordered, as a "world" in the meaning developed by Heidegger in *Being and Time*: as the entirety of existences important for us people (and *ergo* significant) and the relations between them, from astral bodies and mountain ranges, the meaning of which seems independent of our definition understanding them, through intersubjective creations such as political institutions or works of art, to unique mystical experiences that only some are given to have. This sense is a human project, but a project that is not entirely arbitrary as it has ensued from the meeting of existence and man, a project whose usefulness must be confirmed in such an encounter. This sense is a result of the "meeting" of the reality existing independently of man with man understood as a biological species, which as a result of acquiring language and self-awareness has "distinguished itself," i.e. achieved a relative independence from its biological nature and from the natural world surrounding it, *ergo* it has broken free of the reign of purely natural determinism.

Its freedom has become a fact that no cognitivist theories are capable of challenging, while proof in favour of this "fact of freedom" (Kant) is not only our awareness of freedom, as rightly emphasised by Dilthey (awareness given in the act of attributing oneself with responsibility for one's own deeds or failure to act), but also the necessity of adding to the explanation of human behaviour – alongside the concept of causative reason (the foundation of explanations in the natural sciences) – the concept of the deliberate cause, i.e. taking into account human motivations, plans and values.[20]

Firstly, this freedom is freedom from the exclusivity of biological determination (the explicitness of reaction guided by instinct), negative freedom that transforms into freedom towards possessing a world. As Gadamer writes: "To have a world means to have an orientation (Verhalten) toward it. To have an orientation towards the world, however, means to keep oneself so free from what one encounters of the world that one can present it to oneself as it is. This capacity is at once to have a world and to have language. The concept of *world* is thus opposed to the concept of *environment*, which all living beings in the world possess"[21]. It is that freedom that brings into being culture, an essential part of which is morality. Its birth is reflected well, at least in the outline, in the description that Dilthey undertook.

[20] This is shown with competence and insight by Zdzisław Krasnodębski in his book *Rozumienie ludzkiego zachowania*, PIW, Warsaw 1986.

[21] H.-G. Gadamer, *Truth and Method*, Bloomsbury Academic, London 2004, p. 460.

Culture is the entirety of interpretative constructs regulating human life, ones that man living in and in accordance with this culture must share in order for it to be able to survive. He must reproduce and process these constructs, as this is the condition for their essentially symbolic existence. As such enormous responsibility was placed on the naked biologicality of man for sustaining the existence of everything of value to him, everything that determines his "ontological dignity," grasped brilliantly in Heidegger's statement that rocks, trees, horses, angels and even God *are*, but only man exists.[22] Even if it does prove hard for hermeneutic philosophy to acquire universal consent in regard to the claim that the existence of trees or planets depends (in terms of sense) on the human "projecting of being,"[23] it can probably count on acceptance of the assertion that state and law, that art and science, vanish at the moment when people cease to believe in their sense, cease to care for them, i.e. to acknowledge them as important forms in which their existence takes place and is expressed.

Morality is a part of this great and impressive symbolic whole. Myth was also a part of it, yet although – as shown by the works of the likes of Cassirer, Leszek Kołakowski and Ricoeur – it has not vanished entirely from the lives of the people of today, its presence and power of influence has been almost entirely minimised. Today also we are witness to the demise of art in the classical meaning of this word, constitutive for which is the coming into being of the work of art, constituting – as Gadamer so wonderfully put it – an "increase in being" (*Zuwachs am Sein*). This shows the fragility of symbolic creations that surround man, and unveils the fact that even great symbolic forms can vanish or restrict their validity – such as, for example, opera – to a small cluster of aficionados or "followers." Does morality stand before a similar challenge, before a similar threat? This question is by no means as absurd as it may seem at first glance.

Morality emerged initially as decency so as to regulate the coexistence of people in keeping with the professed worldview binding in a given cultural community. Encounters, rivalry between, and the clashes of different cultures generated transformations of morality reflected brilliantly by Gadamer's concept of the fusion (melting) of horizons (*Horizontenverschmeltzung*). It gradually

[22] Cf. M. Heidegger, *What is Metaphysics? Introduction*, transl. M. Groth (https://wagner.edu/psychology/files/2013/01/Heidegger-What-Is-Metaphysics-Translation-GROTH.pdf), p. 77: "Rocks,trees, horses, angels and God are, but none of them exist. Only the human kind of be-ing exists."

[23] Cf. in this aspect John Searle's comment in *Mind, Language and Society*, Basic Books 2008: "I once debated a famous ethnomethodologist who claimed to have shown that astronomers actually create quasars and other astronomical phenomena. 'Look,' I said, 'suppose you and I go for a walk in the moonlight, and I say: "Nice moon tonight," and you agree. Are we creating the moon?' 'Yes,' he said."

turned out that this could be grasped as a universalisation, at least step-by-step, of norms and values, while Christianity provided a particular impulse towards this. However, it did not apply to all cultural circles to the same degree, as the great non-Christian cultures of Asia were still on the battlefield. In relation to Europe and the cultures of both Americas inspired by it, this universalising trend in the growth of morality culminated in the German philosophy of the Enlightenment. Thinkers such as Kant or Fichte, but also Hegel, revealed the possibility of reconciliation – based on the ethical foundation created by Christian religion – of diverse ethical projects with modern ethics, accentuating the rationality and autonomy of the individual as a person, and thus as an existence endowed with dignity as a certain ontological distinguishing factor.

The Nietzschean announcement of the "death of God" was the beginning of the end for this symbiosis of philosophical ethics and religious ethics. The effect is such that each of them is in danger of fading away. Religiously motivated ethics remains important for a constantly shrinking portion of the population, while the rest seem totally bewildered.[24] Because since there is no God, then apparently everything is allowed. However, there are definitely some who while on the one hand are not prepared to submit to the dogmatic decisions of religion (if only because they are unable to accept the two-worldly metaphysics standing behind it), do not on the other hand accept the postmodernist *anything goes*, as they recognise the need for a certain organising of social life that would protect it from total chaos. It is to this group and only this group that philosophical ethics, and also hermeneutical ethics, directs its message. We should have no illusions that it is otherwise. Therefore hermeneutical ethics has two tasks: it must enter a dialogue with religious ethics in order to elaborate something along the lines of a pact of non-aggression, based on what is common to both: the existence in man of something that was formerly termed spirituality. On the other hand it must enter a dialogue with the nihilists and the amoralists, so as to attempt to convince them that "it is worth being ethical."

The latter is neither pointless nor devoid of chances for success. It is not pointless, because in a situation where – on the one hand – there are no general moral pointers at all behind which would stand some unchallenged figure of authority, and – on the other – the proverbial voice of conscience has gone utterly silent, then we are threatened by an ethical atrophy by which all significant regulations regarding human coexistence are delegated to legal or *quasi*-legal decisions, e.g. in the form of occupational ethics, usually drawn

[24] The example of our country shows that participation in religious ceremonies (e.g. attending Sunday masses, church holidays) should not necessarily be treated as living according to the recommendations of an ethics promoted within the religion in question.

up in a form resembling a code. Morality is then relegated to an "ecological niche" (or, better, an existential one), thus becoming – one could say, relating to late Wittgenstein – a "rarely played language game," in which there are ever fewer players, since it does not lead to worldly success. Yet, as Ferdinand Fellmann says: "Auch in der Moral nichts ist so erfolgreich wie der Erfolg."[25]

This will happen if, using Kantian terminology, we reduce morality to legality. Or once having admitted ethicality (as an element of care about oneself) as an existential possibility, we also acknowledge that it is one of many "forms of life," such as practising painting, playing a sport, or showing interest in a certain type of knowledge, i.e. when we place it within the realm of totally free choice, and thus discretion. It will then exist in the image of a Christmas tree decoration, distinguishing certain representatives of *homo sapiens*.

I think that not only those who deal with morality on a professional basis would like to avoid such an alternative. However, a consequence must be a rethinking of the situation in which not only contemporary ethics finds itself, but also morality itself, while there should also be an attempt at an appropriate reaction to it, i.e. in keeping with the demands of the time. This must be an attempt responding to the postmodernist "cut," not with a simple return to pre-critical metaphysics (not only the metaphysics of ideas or substances, but also the metaphysics of "hidden forces"), but by basing on the concepts and formulations developed by hermeneutic philosophy. This signifies drawing up a conception that draws conclusions from Nietzschean perspectivism, from Cassirer's symbolism and Simmel's functionalism, but above all from Heidegger's hermeneutics of factuality, for which the existential of understanding, understood not as a cognitive operation within the humanistic sciences but as a manner of being, distinguishing man from other living creatures, is fundamental.

And therefore what we have to accept is the fragility of the phenomenon known as morality in societies that have experienced the "death of God." If, despite this, we care for the survival of morality and, with it, of moral awareness, then we must investigate the conditions for the possibility of this survival in the situation we are currently dealing with, which is highly unfavourable for it. One has to start with an answer to the fundamental question of what is morality. A good starting point here could be a consideration of the issue of what is the source of duty.

---

[25] Cf. F. Fellmann, *Die Angst des Ethiklehrers vor der Klasse. Ist Moral lehrbar?*, Reclam, Stuttgart 2000, p. 107. This paradoxical sentence may be translated as follows: "And so in morality as well, nothing motivates as well as success."

Where does duty come from?

We owe Kant for the valuable distinguishing into what is legal and what is moral. Legality (*Legalität*) is the area of principles regulating human behaviour in which the criterion for belonging to this area is ordinary obedience that can be intersubjectively ascertained, conforming to rules even if the source of one's motivation here is the fear of punishment for violating them. This sphere is embodied the most fully by the law, upheld by an appropriately formalised judicature. Morality (*Moralität*) in turn is that sphere of actions in which motivation comprises respect for rules, an inner conviction that abiding by them is in keeping with the idea of humanity, a distinguishing factor of which is the autonomous legislation of reason. However, this dichotomous division, set by the exacting criteria of morality adopted by Kant, is insufficient for an adequate grasp of the phenomena in play here.

This is because it seems important in this context to differentiate morality from ethicality, despite these phenomena accompanying each other.[26] If we accept that social life is governed by rules (principles) that cannot be fully translated into the language of legislation, then these rules may be defined as moral, and their entirety – as the prevalent morality. Their observance is controlled by the society that subscribes to them and considers them favourable for its unimpeded and smooth functioning. One may talk about complying with such rules in the third person, i.e. without inquiring as to the individual, subjective motivations of this observance. Norms such as respect for others, truthfulness, not having an inclination for intrigue or slandering others, or finally being guided by a sense of justice can function excellently even when not vouched for by an inner voice of conscience. It is sufficient to have respect for one's own culture, one's tradition, for one's community – and to fear the sanctions from the latter for violating the norms adopted, including exclusion from this community. Moral awareness then signifies an awareness of the principles, norms and values of the world in which one lives, while the will to observe them derives from common sense. However, for such an order to function there has to be morally effective supervision by the community over the individuals, which is really only possible in small groups. In a modern, industrialised, big-city society such control is difficult, or downright illusory, not to mention the illusory nature of the sanctions. Hence the growing trend

[26] I believe that Dilthey's ethical research entitles us to bring in this subtle differentiation; his genealogy of morality, a lot more dependable than that proposed by Nietzsche, *implicite* contains just such a distinction. It is grounded on analysis of the process of the emergence and development of moral awareness, the culmination (and not essence) of which is conscience.

for a growing number of these regulations to take on written form – as legal codes or codes of ethics.

Ethicality differs from morality thus understood in that the first-person perspective is unavoidable and essential for its understanding. Let us try to elucidate it by posing the fundamental question: where does duty in the world come from? As Fellmann rightly claims, "I should" (in the sense of: I'm obliged to) arrives in the world together with "I want."[27] However, this "I want" is not an ordinary animal desire, but represents the will for life, which – apart from extreme cases (concentration camps, the gulags) – in a manner of speaking automatically transcends the ordinary will of experiencing towards the will for a decent, "good" life, i.e. for a happy life. Despite all of his scepticism towards eudaimonism, even Kant claims in his *Critique of Practical Reason* that: "To be happy is a necessary demand of every rational being who is also finite (*endlichen*), and hence an unavoidable determination basis of his desire capacity."[28] This means that he considered happiness not one of many goals that man aspires to, but as a goal *par excellance*, as the profound essence of determining goals at all. Human wanting – because of it being related to awareness, to imagination (presentation) of a goal – had come to be usually termed as will.

Duty on the other hand is a kind of compulsion that derives from the human will thus understood. It is – one could say – a command that will expresses in relation to a specific human individual. Ethical duty is a specific variety of such a relation. It is the kind of feeling of being obliged regarding something, in which the compulsion derives from our own will. Its source is not – as it could be in the case of legality and morality – some kind of external authority (the state, the police, one's peer group, parents), having at its disposal the appropriate sanctions, but an internal compulsion flowing from our own depths. Yet its character is different than in the case of the compulsion, also internal, linked for example to alcoholism, drug addiction or sexoholism. After all, where the abuse of stimulants is concerned we are aware of acting against our own knowledge, and this consciousness suggests to us that we should not do it. But in the case of that internal compulsion commanding us to abide by ethical commitments, a compulsion most often described as one's conscience, then our action is in line with our knowledge regarding what action is right (favourable) for us.

Therefore ethical duty stands out from the remaining social commitments in that its basis is the following relation: in conscience, the one obliged and the

---

[27] Cf. F. Fellmann, *Wie das Sollen in die Welt kommt. Ein Plädoyer für Moralpsychologie*, "Deutsche Zeitschrift für Philosophie" 3/2003, Berlin, p. 491.

[28] I. Kant, *The Critique of Practical Reason*, transl. P. McPherson Rudisill, posted 2012, http://kantwesley.com/Kant/CritiqueOfPracticalReason.pdf, p. 27.

one obliging are one and the same person. The relation between theory and practice is also striking in the case of ethical norms. Because the task of norms is to motivate actions, a symbiosis occurs between theory and practice that hinders, or in fact even renders impossible, a purely theoretical consolidation of morality. Such justification certainly cannot adopt the form of rational command, deriving from the fact of human rationality and freedom, generating as it were an ethical stance. The fact of the existence of will – which Kant's brilliant successor, Schopenhauer, knew perfectly – cannot be bypassed, marginalised or avoided. Which is why one should look for the foundations of conscience not in the transcendental theory of subjectivity, but rather in anthropology and psychology, which thematise our human motivations in the context of aspiring for a fulfilled life. That "wanting" is "awarded" to us, i.e. it does not belong to the sphere of discretion, of our choice. "Anybody can want what they want, but nobody can not want to want."[29] Because, as Martin Heidegger writes, we are thrown into existing, or simply: we have to be.

Indicating happiness as the main motive of our activities naturally evokes associations with hedonism. This is why it must be pointed out that the concept of happiness transcends ordinary animal pleasure. After all, it may be recognised as a reflective concept: its scope goes beyond momentary delight, and indicates will and consciousness of the lasting of some kind of state. Contemplation of the conditions of a happy life also leads our investigation beyond the area of action – towards an acting person aspiring for happiness. But this is not the *ego cogito* of rationalistic idealistic philosophy, since there we will not rediscover motivation for acting. The will to live, constituting the anthropological core of the aspiration for happiness, is articulated not only in goals and in the actions leading to them, but above all in human stances and attitudes. Man, as an *animal symbolicum* (i.e. a hermeneutic being), is an ontological curiosity, because his existence depends on his consciousness, i.e. not only does the existence define consciousness (as Marx would have it), but also consciousness defines existence.

Every one of us generates a certain image of ourselves, an image that alongside facts regarding our birth and life to date also contains diverse interpretations. Without this, we would feel like pawns in a game being played by somebody else, and not like people capable of taking our own independent actions in keeping with our self-understanding, with the image of our own self. This image is tied dialectically to our vision of man in general. It also translates into the claims for importance and recognition that we put before others. Thanks to the image of man, we interpret our will for living in keeping

[29] F. Fellmann, *Wie das Sollen...*, op. cit., p. 492 [transl. from the Polish – J. Weber].

with our sense of or desire for personal identity. This is why our self-image is, essentially, the "will-towards-being-oneself."[30] However, this "self" is not always fully revealed in our actions, the confirmation of which is the question we sometimes face from people observing our actions but unable to understand them: "What do you really want?"

The significance of others' recognition is manifested for example in the fact that we feel stabbed to our very depths when somebody, instead of only rebuking our specific behaviour (or behaviours), which we are usually able to understand and accept, criticises our entire life attitude. Then we feel as though somebody has pulled the ground away from under our feet, and sometimes react very emotionally. On occasion we ourselves are the source of such criticism of our own stance in life, when disgusted by our deeds – not reflecting our image of ourselves – we find the honesty and courage to criticise ourselves, so as to transform the deep disappointment we feel towards ourselves into a source of spiritual transformation and renewal. This shows that, as Scheler pertinently wrote, it is not so much that one is always a person as that one becomes one, i.e. a person is not some kind of substantial magnitude, but a result of interpretations: of self-appraisal mediated by the judgment of others, as long as they are people we acknowledge as free, as our equals, and worthy of respect. This is because happiness also comprises the "qualified consent" (approval) of others, which we need in order to recognise ourselves as morally justified people, and thanks to this – to cope with the "without-ground" (absence of rationale) of our will to live. That we are sometimes indifferent to what others think of us results from the fact that those "others" do not always have to be specific others. As a rule it is precisely not some concrete but some imagined and generalised (idealised) Other who constitutes the point of reference for our self-image and our self-appraisal.

Because philosophical literature is dominated by a one-sided, hedonistic grasp of happiness, falling into one of two extremes tends to be the result: the defence of pure hedonism, or its firm rejection, for example in the form of the negation of will as we see in Schopenhauer. This leads to a non-consideration of such aspects (possibilities) of a deeper experiencing of happiness, such as are its (long-) lastingness and social mediation, which – after all – determine the full sense of this notion. This brings to mind the almost obtrusive thought that "ethical rationality" is determined by the will to belong to a certain moral community (for example to Kant's "realm of ends"). However, non-ethicality is not measured then – as Kant would like – by the logical contradiction in the area of maxims, but by the absurdity of will devoid of a subjective point of reference: of respect on the part of the imagined or factual other.

[30] Ibidem, p. 494.

Ethical duty therefore derives from the will of the self, the will that imposes restrictions on our whims. The source of these restrictions in turn is the acknowledgement of others as moral entities equal to us. It is on them that our sense of our own value depends. "Our latent need for acceptance is expressed in duty, a need that cannot be forced but that can be expected when we display towards others the respect due to them as autonomous entities. Duty may therefore be considered objectivised wanting, and more precisely – the border of our will's power over others."[31] Despite scepticism towards the rationalistic character of Kant's ethics one cannot but notice that the grasp of the ethical commitment and conscience here contains elements that are close to his grasp: "taking into account an imagined other in one's own wanting transforms teleological rationality into a form of sagacity that could be described as intersubjective self-legislation."[32] It could also be recognised as a sublime articulation of the Golden Rule, whose presence in Kant's thinking – as we indicated in another chapter of this book – was noticed by Ricoeur. Interestingly, it is also close to utilitarianism, although not so much its interpretation encountered most often, i.e. the utilitarianism of actions, but rather the oft-omitted utilitarianism of rules, according to which universal happiness cannot be achieved at the cost of an individual's happiness. In John Stuart Mill, a classic of this direction, we also find an explanation of where we get the strength from to realise moral duties even when they are incompatible with our egoistic tendencies. After all others' recognition may sometimes prove too weak, abstract or distant, while we experience the suppression of our desires – due to compliance to the Golden Rule – as a certain unpleasantness. A way out of this dilemma, as Mill has already done, is the introduction of two types of pleasure. One may then argue in favour of the claim that we do not perceive restrictions resulting from the adoption of an ethical stance as purely unpleasant, since the renunciation of immoral actions generates within us a positive feeling of our own value, which "communicates" with our Will of Us Ourselves, with the deepest layers of personal life linked to our vision of a "truly human existence." We feel this as a sense of pride in ourselves that fills us with happiness, and sometimes even as a sense of moral superiority.

The existence of not only sensory (carnal) but also spiritual pleasures leads to us being ready to surrender the former, since the reward for this will be an increase in the latter. This of course requires the elementary skill of consideration, thanks to which we care for our own "economy of feelings." Therefore reducing the aspiration for happiness to just naked, hedonistic egoism would be a blatant, a priori simplification. The elasticity of the human experiencing

[31] Ibidem, p. 496.

[32] Ibidem, p. 497.

of pleasure enables the functioning of ethical brakes, which can lead to the experiencing of pleasure flowing from a sense of one's own dignity and value. On the condition, quite naturally, that this applies to somebody who wants to be a person, i.e. somebody who possesses the minimum of what has sometimes been described in the history of philosophy as the "moral sense." Where this is entirely absent, it is also hard to find a moral entity, and thus hard to reflect over oneself. In such a case only therapy or elementary ethical education may help. Its purpose is to replace the hitherto limited and educated self-image with one that also takes into account lasting forms of happiness, resulting from a receptivity for experiencing spiritual pleasures.

It is worth emphasising, though, that the derivation of duty from one's own will, presented but in outline above, also opens up towards the so-called material ethics of value, but modifying its self-understanding (interpretation) somewhat, i.e. rejecting the theory of an a priori, meaning supra-historical, validity of the defined catalogue and defined structure of value (from which the appropriate life norms are then derived). What is understood as the conditioning of individual happiness may be expressed as a collection of historically variable values constituting the content of morality of a given era or cultural community. This in turn makes it possible to talk about something such as a "moral culture" of a given community, and even – though with great caution – about the ethical progress taking place within it. This progress would involve people learning to set higher demands before themselves thanks to the increase in the significance ascribed in it to spiritual pleasures. As Fellmann rightly observes, exhortations alone appealing to honesty in action are insufficient if they do not appeal to our self-understanding, if they do not evoke within us a more realistic image of ourselves and do not show (through argument or not) the impropriety of such a vision of man as we adopt consciously or subconsciously. Only an emotional jolt can cause the appropriate transformation in attitudes and behaviour. It is difficult for us to belittle the pressure on self-image, as our sense of identity and dignity is threatened here.

The shaping of moral awareness

Ethical education does not therefore have to mean the boring teaching to somebody of "moral tablets" (a collection of commands and prohibitions) that must be observed from then on, or the analysing of so-called moral *casussen* (more ambitious in intent, yet frequently just as abstract). It should show and emphasise the significance of self-fulfilment as the will of being oneself, support the building of one's self-image, and teach the tearing down of the curtains that we unfurl before ourselves in order to justify our own unethical behaviours. Such upbringing is also always self-upbringing. Above all it requires courage. For it to be effective the upbringer must be faithful to what is conveyed to those being brought up, in keeping with the specificity of ethical knowledge delineated by the relations of theory and practice. This is because nothing is more counterproductive that an upbringer disregarding the principles he is meant to convey to others. "Colloquial moral knowledge is evoked by tradition and models, although just like any colloquial knowledge it also seeks benefit, success, and recognition from others."[33]

However, a radical separation of communicative behaviour and instrumental behaviour, aimed at achieving a specific goal, would seem risky since moral awareness also seems to be developing in regard to the goal of a fulfilled and happy life in a respectful community. The fact that this is a more long-term goal makes no difference, meaning that here as well practice in certain techniques of thinking, acting, cooperating, communicating intentions towards others and even in generating certain habits that are valued positively is useful. As Rainer Fuchs quite rightly stated, learning is the motor of cultural evolution.[34] Morality as a set of rules governing the coexistence of the population is part of this evolution, and as such it is something obvious that these rules require assimilation, nurturing and passing on to others in the form of teaching.

A given morality – as we have already pointed out – retains its force and freshness when people want to live in keeping with its recommendations, and when they also want to pass it on to their children and grandchildren. This teaching should be free of elements of dogmatism, as otherwise it frequently leads – as Richard M. Hare noticed – to the creation of "inflexible ethical intuitionists,"[35] fundamentalists incapable of adjusting their own moral judgments and behaviour do the changing situations. As for the teaching, which needs to be stressed here once again, it is not achieved by conveying a certain skill, the usage of which by the learner is of indifference to the teacher, but through examples and practical guidelines (advice), which clarify and concretise the ethical principles conveyed. The generating of certain habits, ethically beneficial to both the individual and the community, is a significant component of the upbringing. Generating positive habits is closely tied to social education. However, it does not have to remain at variance with the individual's right to self-definition, as it most often applies to persons who have not yet reached full social maturity (or whose current "self-understanding" eliminates them from the community that, despite this, they would like to belong to).

---

[33] B. Irrgang, *Praktische Ethik...*, op. cit., p. 135 [transl. from the Polish – J. Weber].

[34] Cf. R. Fuchs, *Einführung in die Lernpsychologie*, Wissenschaftliche Buchgesellschaft, Darmstadt 1991 (2nd edition), p. 40.

[35] Cf. R.M. Hare, *Moralisches Denken: seine Ebenen, seine Methode, sein Witz*, Suhrkamp Verlag, Frankfurt am Main 1992, p. 103.

Upbringing as communication of the culture or tradition of a particular moral community leads to the creation of "preliminary knowledge" (the hermeneutic *Vorwissen*), the existence of which enables cognitive and emotional access to a given phenomenal sphere, and in this case – to the ethical sphere. Not only hermeneutically-oriented ethicists, such as Irrgang, but also that classic of ethics, Kant, emphasise the particular kind of circular character of the phenomenon of morality: argumentative effectiveness regarding ethical judgment, e.g. criticism of somebody for not fulfilling a duty that they have assumes the adoption of an ethical stance at least (positive receptivity towards morality).

It is for these reasons that hermeneutic ethics does not try to create new systems of normative ethics. It refers rather to existing morality, which in the form of the ethos functioning within a given community may be raised to a level of higher awareness, improved, and adapted to the evolving and historically determined "situation of man." This may be illustrated with Gadamer's brilliant assertion, admittedly regarding philosophy but one that may be carried over to hermeneutical ethics – that philosophical thought involves making what everybody knows somewhat more conscious.

Hermeneutical ethics is a situational ethics, relating to pre-existing moral awareness that takes into account the world of life (*Lebenswelt*) that it is related to. However, it is not a conservative ethics subscribing to traditionalism. There is a critical moment contained in it that derives from the situation in which people ascertain that hitherto practices and their related principles fail when coming up against new phenomena.

The circular character of ethical knowledge

Hermeneutic ethics believes that the manner of functioning of social morality is oscillation (*Hin- und Herbewegung* – as Irrgang writes[36]) between what is situationally-concrete (a demand of action posed by the situation) and the general ethical rule that we already have, and that is modified and enriched in meaning by every new, creative application. This oscillation was worked out brilliantly by Gadamer, which I wrote about in the chapter devoted to him. This is not obsessive criticism, suspecting the existence of oppression in every morality, which therefore has to be brought before an arbitrary and enlightened tribunal of a historically understood rationality, but critique referring to historical reason, constituting the sum of the historical experiences of people and peoples. In keeping with hermeneutic philosophy, any new knowledge

[36] B. Irrgang, *Praktische Ethik...*, op. cit., p. 28.

is rooted in the old. Sometimes a given morality, functioning reasonably well to date, has difficulty coming up with solutions for new problems that have emerged, for example as a result of the growing technicalisation of our lives. Then its correction is essential. But then also – as Irrgang notes rightly in referring *implicite* to Gadamer –innovative actions usually contain numerous typical elements already existing in past ethics.

Morality does not constitute some totally autonomous area wrenched from the entirety of human life practice. In keeping with the hermeneutic claim to universality (*Universalitätsanspruch der Hermeneutik*), derived from the universality of understanding, setting instrumental reason (and the instrumental actions that flow from it) against communicative reason (within which morality and ethics would fit) is not appropriate. There exists one, shared world of life in which people's care of their existence is manifested in the form of diverse actions. An understanding of their character provides a foothold for hermeneutical ethics. "As opposed to cognitivist ethics," says Irrgang, "in keeping with the [hermeneutic] conception of ethical understanding we only understand an ethical duty when we are prepared to fulfil it, as long as other duties do not oppose it. Purely theoretical reflection over it or discerning it is not yet understanding, but is metaethical reflection."[37]

Hermeneutical ethics expresses actions as interpretational constructs. After all they constitute meaningful connections of intentions and deeds defined by a purpose. The dialectic of the objective and subjective sides of the action's sense, or in other words of the first person perspective (me as the acting person) and third person perspective (me as the observer of somebody's action), is constitutive for their understanding. Both depend on interpretation. "That double role, of the doing and the observing, is constitutive for action. As a result of this, a complex and at the same time inseparable connection occurs between the action, as a subjectively designed process of experience, and behaviour, which may be grasped by other people as the embodiment of the action."[38] From a hermeneutic point of view, in the interpretation (understanding) of action one should take into account such aspects as: an analysis of the situation as something given, something objective; an analysis of the motivations (subjective, but also given: characterological and related to worldview); an analysis of the project (as an idea for reaction to a challenge posed by the situation); an analysis of the goal (which the action intends to achieve); an analysis of the means (leading to this goal); and an analysis of the consequences of the action.

[37] Ibidem, p. 95.

[38] Ibidem, p. 97.

Because the world in which we live is the world of our life practice, snatching technical actions from this entirety, to then set them against it and even cause an impression of a threat to human ethicality flowing from here, is wrong. The breakthrough character of *Being and Time* was a result of the starting point it adopted, which was not the pure transcendental awareness generating the "world" in cognitive acts, but the "consciousness" (*Dasein*) entangled in practice in reality, concerned about the world of its life. This was translated into the primacy of the category of *Zuhandenheit*, handiness (and its related tool), over brute existence (*Vorhandenheit*), being the presence of something as an entity in space-time. This seemed to create for hermeneutic thought an original and highly promising basis for an integration of technology in the life practices of the *Lebenswelt.* Sadly, Heidegger's late philosophy, which he himself described as the Thinking of Being, abandons these possibilities unveiled in *Sein und Zeit*, creating a philosophy of technology, which – despite the calming declarations of its author – sees a powerful dehumanising factor in the development of modern technology. This is also naturally reflected in the attitude towards ethics, as shown in comments of the type: "Farming is now a motorised food industry, in essence the same as the fabrication of corpses in gas chambers and extermination camps, the same as the blockade and starving of the peasantry, the same as the fabrication of the hydrogen bomb."[39]

In referring to Heidegger, thinkers such as Günther Anders or Zygmunt Bauman made the existence of contemporary technology the motor of dehumanisation of the world in which we have come to live. The latter says that only "a rationally defined world" made the Holocaust something that was possible. "That neutralising, isolating and ignoring was the Nazis' goal when they employed the enormous apparatus of modern industry, transport, science, administration and technology for this task. Without that, the Holocaust would have been unthinkable [...]."[40] In a technical sense perhaps this was so, but that does not explain the significance of motivation deriving from a vision of reality that enabled the implementation of technology of that kind. It leads to a demonization of technology and a minimisation of the significance of the sphere of world view. By tossing together the gulags on the one hand and Hiroshima on the other, Bauman misses the fact that the former was but loosely connected to the development of technology, while the latter – unquestionably impossible without highly developed technology – was not linked to attempts at creating a new man. As such it had no support in ethical self-interestedness (e.g. racial or class chauvinism).

[39] M. Heidegger, *Das Ge-Stell*, in idem, *Bremer und Freiburger Vorträge*, ed. P. Jaeger, *Gesamtausgabe*, vol. 79, Vittorio Klostermann, Frankfurt am Main 2005, p. 53.

[40] Z. Bauman, *Nowoczesność i Zagłada* [Modernity and the Holocaust], transl. F. Jaszuński, Fundacja Kulturalna Masada, Warsaw 1992, p. 259.

According to Bauman the rationalism of the modern society, because of functionalisation and thereby the depersonalisation of interpersonal relations, renders the prevalence of ethical relations impossible. However, he misses the teachings flowing from the thinking of Hegel, who ordered that a given society's solidarity be sought not in individual charity, but in the creation of institutions providing care for the weakest links in social life. As such Bauman does not notice that the hiatus linked to a reduction in moral personal bonds may be filled by other normative aspects of social life – on the condition, however, that the sources of ethical reflection that cannot be replaced by the Heideggerian expectation for a new Missive of Being that tells us how to live "above ontology and ethics" do not run dry. Bauman admittedly chooses a slightly different solution, but it is equally as dissatisfactory as Heidegger's. He refers to Levinas as the greatest moral philosopher of the 20th century.

"Because Bauman believes," writes Rolf Zimmermann, "that modern society, because of its functional impersonality and mechanisms of distance-creating demoralisation right up to "killing at a distance," leaves no room for autonomous individual morality, then contrary to the sociological *mainstream* he insists that the ability to differentiate evil from good should be sought in a certain non-social endowment of man that would have to be comparable to his "biological constitution" and achievable only via "human proximity."'[41] This solution is dissatisfactory for a few reasons. We have already discussed some of these in the chapter on Ricoeur. The transformation of "any other" into a "close other," into "my brother," is only possible on the basis of a religious stance, which – if only in regard to the "escape of the gods" proclaimed by Heidegger – is not something universal even among people considering themselves believers.

No less important a reason behind the weakness of this proposition is the asymmetric character of the relationship on which it is based. This makes the conditions of recognition and reciprocity – constitutive for the existence of morality in the full meaning of the word – immaterial. Moreover, the face of the Other may prove an alternative not only misleading, but even threatening, because – as Rolf Zimmermam, who criticises Bauman, writes – "it may also assume the features of the Arctic cold or a readiness to commit mass murder. The strength of the morality with which that must be opposed cannot derive solely from love without reason."[42] Unconditional love for thy neighbour, one could add, is not some kind of source-like phenomenon, but a historical phenomenon tied to the emergence of Christianity. And only a renaissance of this religion and the permeation of this theme it has into other religions would give rise to hope for the accomplishment of Bauman's utopia.

---

[41] R. Zimmermann, *Moral als Macht...*, op. cit., p. 94 [transl. from the Polish – J. Weber].

[42] Ibidem, p. 95.

The goals of a hermeneutical ethics

Let us return to hermeneutics. According to Bernhard Irrgang, a hermeneutical ethics that focuses on practical application has two main tasks. The first is to raise individual competences in regard to self-control, self-reflection and responsible action via a kind of "polishing" of one's conscience (perfecting of one's moral awareness). The second task is reflection over such social frameworks as the political, legal, economic and mass-media orders that constitute the stage for human ethical actions, and either facilitate them or hinder them, by rewarding immoral actions. Hermeneutical ethics attaches a great deal of importance to the accomplish ability of ethical demands. It opts for ethical realism; although it appreciates the significance of ethical heroism (of so-called supererogation), it does not demand this of ordinary mortals. It treats declarations of the kind: "you should, so you can, and you even must" as absurd. Which is not to say that it marginalises the role of personal moral models. Quite the opposite: *Weltbilder und Leitbilder* – visions of the world and personal models constitute a kind of dynamic foundation in hermeneutical ethics, a foundation that one can refer to in the formation of moral judgments on which moral education may be built.

These two fundamental tasks are joined by a third task, one for which hermeneutics seems to be specially predestined. As Rorty expressed in his famous work *Philosophy and the Mirror of Nature*, this is the task of the translator mediating between discourses and making it possible to achieve first of all mutual understanding, and then agreement. In the case of ethics, the task of the hermeneutist is to "embrace assessments and values in ethically motivated discourses with conflict management."[43] Hermeneutical ethics seems particularly predestined for this job, because it is neither fundamentalist ethics nor an ethical relativism or nihilism. It does not acknowledge as true the assertion expressed in the title of Otfried Höffe's book, that "morality is the price of modernity," but is aware of the challenge for morality posed by the late-modern social reality, in which the aestheticisation of ethics leads to its transformation to such an extent that what is good and right becomes confused with what is nice and original, even if – in moral categories – it is outrageous or repulsive.[44] Hermeneutical ethics has no ambition of consolidating ethics. It rather sees itself as action towards the protection and development of an

---

[43] B. Irrgang, *Praktische Ethik...*, op. cit., p. 177.

[44] Cf. O. Höffe, *Moral als Preis der Moderne. Ein Versuch über Wissenschaft, Technik und Umwelt*, Suhrkamp Verlag, Frankfurt am Main 1993.

ethos appropriate for the times in which we live.[45] Contrary to Nietzsche, it claims that moral facts do exist, although they are the result of the adoption of certain interpretational assumptions, just like physical or biological facts. The interpretational character of morality is – in comparison to this (what Abel showed) – even stronger. As the Austrican ethicist Malte Hossenfelder rightly observes:

"Morality is obviously no empirical concept, such as a cow, a star or water, and it takes no account of things we find in nature. Admittedly it is if one has views, and thus a certain psychic phenomenon, in mind. But this is not what constitutes the object of ethics. It is this as a value, as something that people wish for and something that can influence their actions, and as a valuating concept it is undoubtedly something "made by people themselves." A certain defined view is subjected to valuation, while its objects – e.g. law or social help – are not something that people would find as ready in the world, because they created these concepts in order for them to help regulate how one treats oneself. These concepts cannot be interpreted from our behaviour, and they only exist in our thinking, due to which an observer from a world alien to ours would be unable to understand them."[46]

For Hossenfelder it is obvious that a consequence of the fact that norms, and together with them all practical concepts, are in this sense non-empirical (despite embodying certain institutions available to empirical studies), is that one cannot obtain cognitive access to them via ordinary observation, as in the case of the astronomical observation of distant planets. "Another method, and namely "understanding," is also necessary. This is because these institutions only exist in our minds, where they have been spontaneously created."[47]

Kant consolidated ethics on the basis of deliberations over the essence and purpose of man, while Mill and Dilthey derived its sense from its genesis: the function of regulating social life, leading to better self-fulfilment, greater happiness. Hermeneutic philosophy foregoes such consolidation, although it discerns valuable and important aspects of both these approaches. Its issue is rather concern about morality realised through the ethical realism deriving from the existing moral order (ethos). Hermeneutical ethics is an ethics embracing reflection over the conditions of individual self-fulfilment in a social and natural context.[48] It constitutes a combination of individualistic ethics and social ethics, as it has to combine the ideal of self-fulfilment ("the well-guarded autonomy

[45] Cf. B. Irrgang, *Praktische Ethik...*, op. cit., p. 124.

[46] M. Hossenfelder, *Der Wille zum Recht und das Streben nach Glück. Grundlegung einer Ethik des Wollens*, C.H. Beck, München 2000, p. 145 [transl. from the Polish – J. Weber].

[47] Ibidem, p. 36.

[48] Cf. B. Irrgang, *Hermeneutische Ethik...*, op. cit., p. 74.

of the individual") with the ideal of an order based on the existence of pro-social moral strengths. Therefore, where the political dimension is concerned, it is a combination of democracy, liberalism and republicanism. As such it cannot be positioned on a rigid axis of left-wing – right-wing, or progressive (permissive) – conservative. In the place of incontrovertible principles (such as reason or happiness) from which one may then, *more geometrico*, derive moral norms, it introduces thinking in pluralistically understood categories of "ethical paradigms," relating to "worlds of life."

Hermeneutical ethics, as Gerhard Pfafferott rightly ascertains, finds the foundation of ethicality in the already functioning morality, in the historically and culturally manifesting "moral styles."[49] Ethicality is sought in that form of human rationality that is not limited to self-awareness or intellect, but which relates to the need for self-reflection, also embracing the emotional and axiological spheres. However, ethical self-reflection has its roots in interpretational life practice, the historically determined character of which is hard to challenge. Forms of life – characteristic *telos* – existing in public space become the most important points of reference, but ones that are not immune to criticism coming from the perspective of ethicality. Such criticism facilitates the elaboration of a formula that can constitute a foothold for such an act of questioning recognition. A good basis here would seem to be the principle developed by Ricoeur that one should aspire for "*aiming at the 'good life' with and for others, in just institutions.*"[50] This expresses the fundamental elements of the ethical phenomenon in a terse manner requiring a new interpretation on every occasion, while retaining a formal character that does not exclude anybody.

[49] Cf. G. Pfafferott, *Ethik und Hermeneutik...*, op. cit., p. 249 et seq.

[50] P. Ricoeur, *Oneself as Another*, University of Chicago Press, Chicago and London 1994, p. 172.

Bibliography

Abel G., "Interpretationsphilosophie. Kommentare und Repliken," *Deutsche Zeitschrift für Philosophie* No. 44, 1996.

Abel G., *Interpretationswelten. Gegenwartsphilosophie jenseits vom Essentialismus und Relativismus*, Suhrkamp Verlag, Frankfurt am Main 1993.

Abel G., *Nietzsche. Die Dynamik des Willen zur Macht und die ewige Wiederkehr*, Berlin – New York 1984.

Abel G., *Sprache, Zeichen, Interpretation*, Suhrkamp Verlag, Frankfurt am Main 1999.

Abel G., *Zeichen der Wirklichkeit*, Suhrkamp Verlag Frankfurt am Main 2004.

Abel G., "Zeichen- und Interpretationsethik," in A. Przyłębski (ed.), *Ethik im Lichte der Hermeneutik*, Königshausen & Neumann, Würzburg 2010.

Bauman Z., *Nowoczesność i Zagłada* [Modernity and the Holocaust], transl. F. Jaszuński, Fundacja Kulturalna Masada, Warsaw 1992.

Bottani L., "Przekaz, dialog i komunikacja. Martina Heideggera koncepcja języka," transl. E. Andrzejewska, in B. Andrzejewski (ed.), *Komunikacja – rozumienie – dialog*, Wydawnictwo Naukowe UAM Poznań 1990.

Brogowski L., *Świadomość i historia*, słowo/ obraz terytoria, Gdańsk 2004.

Cullen B., "Heideggers Metaontologie und die Möglichkeit einer philosophischen Ethik," in D. Papenfuss, O. Pöggeler (eds), *Zur philosophischen Aktualität Heideggers*, Klostermann Verlag, Frankfurt am Main 1991, vol. 1.

Dahlstrom D.O., "Seinsvergessenheit oder moralphilosophische Naivität Heideggers Interpretation der praktischen Philosophie Kants," in D. Papenfuss, O. Pöggeler (eds), *Zur philosophischen Aktualität Heideggers*, Klostermann Verlag, Frankfurt am Main 1991, vol. 1.

Descartes R., *Zasady filozofii*, transl. I. Dąmbska, PWN, Warsaw 1960.

Dilthey W., *Gesammelte Schriften*, ed. G. Misch, Bd. VI, Stuttgart – Göttingen 1978.

Dilthey W., "System der Ethik," in idem, *Gesammelte Schriften*, vol. X, Stuttgart – Göttingen 1981.

Dostal R.J., "Eros, Freundschaft und Politik: Heideggers Versagen," in D. Papenfuss, O. Pöggeler (eds), *Zur philosophischen Aktualität Heideggers*, Klostermann Verlag, Frankfurt am Main 1991, vol. 1.

Dreyfus H., *Between Techne and Technology: The Ambiguous Place of Equipment in Being and Time*, Tulane Studies in Philosophy 1984, vol. 332.

Dybel P., "Panie Heidegger, kiedy pan napisze etykę," in P. Marciszuk, C. Wodziński (eds), *Heidegger dzisiaj*, Warsaw 1990.

Fellmann F., *Die Angst des Ethiklehrers vor der Klasse. Ist Moral lehrbar?*, Reclam, Stuttgart 2000.

Fellmann F., *Para. Erotyczne źródła człowieczeństwa*, transl. J. Duraj, W. Małecki, Wydawnictwo Naukowe UAM, Poznan 2009.

Fellmann F., "Wie das Sollen in die Welt kommt. Ein Plädoyer für Moralpsychologie," *Deutsche Zeitschrift für Philosophie* 3/2003, Berlin.

Fuchs R., *Einführung in die Lernpsychologie*, Wissenschaftliche Buchgesellschaft, Darmstadt 1991.

Gadamer H.-G., *A Century of Philosophy: A Conversation with Riccardo Dottori*, Bloomsbury Academic, London 2006.

Gadamer H.-G., "On the Possibility of a Philosophical Ethics," transl. by J. Weinsheimer, in R.E. Palmer (ed.), *The Gadamer Reader. A Bouquet of the Later Writings*, Northwestern University Press, Evanston 2007.

Gadamer H.-G., *Teoria, technika, praktyka*, transl. A. Przyłębski, in A. Przyłębski, *Gadamer*, Wiedza Powszechna, Warsaw 2007.

Gadamer H.-G., *The Idea of the Good in Platonic-Aristotelian Philosophy*, transl. P.Ch. Smith, Yale University Press, New Haven and London 1986.

Gadamer H.-G., *Truth and Method*, Bloomsbury Academic, London 2004.

Gadamer H.-G., "Über die Möglichkeit einer philosophischen Ethik," in idem, *Gesammelte Werke*, Mohr Siebeck, Tübingen 1987.

Hans-Georg Gadamer on Education, Poetry and History, ed. D. Misgeld and G. Nicholson, transl. L. Schmidt and M. Reuss, State University of New York Press, New York 1992.

Hare R.M., *Moralisches Denken: seine Ebenen, seine Methode, sein Witz*, Suhrkamp Verlag, Frankfurt am Main 1992.

Hartmann N., "Problem wartości w filozofii współczesnej," transl. W. Galewicz, in W. Galewicz, *N. Hartmann*, Wiedza Powszechna, Warsaw 1987.

Hegel G.W.F., *Elements of the Philosophy of Right*, transl. H.B. Nisbet, Cambridge University Press, Cambridge2003.

Hegel G.F.W., *Phänomenologie des Geistes*, Suhrkamp, Frankfurt am Main 2008.

Hegel G.W.F., *Wykłady z filozofii dziejów* [Lectures on the History of Philosophy], trans. J. Grabowski and A. Landman, PWN, Warsaw 1958.

Heidegger M., *Being and Time*, transl. J. Stambaugh, State University of New York Press, New York 1996.

Heidegger M., *Contributions to Philosophy*, trans. P. Emad and K. Maly, Indiana University Press, Indiana 1999.

Heidegger M., "Das Ge-Stell," in idem, *Bremer und Freiburger Vorträge*, ed. P. Jaeger, *Gesamtausgabe*, vol. 79, Vittorio Klostermann, Frankfurt am Main 2005.

Heidegger M., "Letter on humanism," trans. F.A. Capuzzi, in *Pathmarks*, Cambridge University Press, Cambridge 1998.

Heidegger M., *What is Metaphysics? Introduction*, transl. M. Groth (https://wagner.edu/psychology/files/2013/01/Heidegger-What-Is-Metaphysics-Translation-GROTH.pdf.

Herman W., *Próba ugruntowania metafizyki*, Oficyna Wydawnicza Politechniki Warszawskiej, Warsaw 2008.

Höffe O., *Moral als Preis der Moderne. Ein Versuch über Wissenschaft, Technik und Umwelt*, Suhrkamp Verlag, Frankfurt am Main 1993.

Horwicz A., *Die Analyse der qualitativen Urteile*, Magdeburg 1878.

Hossenfelder M., *Der Wille zum Recht und das Streben nach Glück. Grundlegung einer Ethik des Wollens*, C.H. Beck, München 2000.

Irrgang B., *Praktische Ethik aus hermeneutischen Sicht*, Schöningh Verlag, Paderborn 1998.

Irrgang B., *Hermeneutische Ethik: Pragmatisch-ethische Orientierung in technologischen Gesellschaften*, Wissenschaftliche Buchgesellschaft, Darmstadt 2012.

Januszkiewicz M., *Etyczny wymiar hermeneutyki (wokół Gianni Vattimo)*, in A.F. Kola, A. Szahaj (ed.), *Filozofia i etyka interpretacji*, Universitas, Cracow 2007.

Jung M., *Dilthey zur Einführung*, Junius Verlag, Hamburg 1996.

Kogge W., *Technologie des 21. Jahrhunderts. Perspektiven der Technikphilosophie*, Deutsche Zeitschrift für Philosophie 6/2008.

Kant I., *Groundwork for the Metaphysics of Morals*, transl. and ed. A.W. Wood, Yale University Press, New Haven and London 2002.

Kant I., *Metafizyka moralności*, trans. E. Nowak, Wydawnictwo Naukowe PWN, Warsaw 2005.

Kant I., *Religion Within the Bounds of Sheer Reason*, transl. P. McPherson Rudisill, posted 2013, http://kantwesley.com/Kant/RationalReligion.pdf.

Kant I., *The Critique of Practical Reason*, transl. P. McPherson Rudisill, posted 2012, http://kantwesley.com/Kant/CritiqueOfPracticalReason.pdf.

Krasnodębski Z., *Rozumienie ludzkiego zachowania*, PIW, Warsaw 1986.

Kuderowicz Z., *Dilthey*, Wiedza Powszechna, Warsaw 1987.

Kuderowicz Z., *Kant*, Wiedza Powszechna, Warsaw 2000.

Küenzlen G., *Der Neue Mensch. Eine Untersuchung zur säkularen Religionsgeschichte der Moderne*, Suhrkamp, Frankfurt am Main 1997.

Hans L., *Filozofia pragmatycznego interpretacjonizmu*, transl. Z. Zwoliński, Oficyna Wydawnicza, Warsaw 1995.

Liptow J., *Zur Rolle der Sprache in Sein und Zeit*, in B. Merker (ed.), *Verstehen nach Heidegger und Brandom*, Meiner Verlag, Hamburg 2009.

Marquard O., *Farewell to Matters of Principle: Philosophical Studies*, Oxford University Press 1989.

Miłosz Cz., *To*, Wyd. Znak, Kraków 2001, pp. 76-77, http://www.poemhunter.com/poem/unde-malum/ [30.11.2016].

Nietzsche F., *Thus Spoke Zarathustra*, ed. B. Chapko, feedbooks, 1(15) *The Thousand and One Goals*.

Nietzsche F., *Twilight of the Idols*, KGA VI.

Nietzsche F., *Werke. Kritische Gesamtausgabe*, vol. 14, eds G. Colli, M. Montinari, De Gruyter, München 1980.

Paczkowska-Łagowska E., *Logos życia*, słowo/ obraz terytoria, Gdańsk 2000.

Pfafferott G., *Hermeneutische Ethik. Pragmatisch-ethische Orientierung in technologischen Gesellschaften*, Wissenschaftliche Buchgesellschaft, Darmstadt 2007.

Pfafferott G., *Ethik und Hermeneutik. Mensch und Moral im Gefüge der Lebensform*, Forum Academicum, Bonn 1981.

Potępa M., *Dialektyka i hermeneutyka w filozofii F.D. Schleiernachera* [Dialectics and Hermeneutics in the Philosophy of F.D. Schleiermacher], Wyd. Uniwersytetu Łódzkiego, Łódź 1992.

Przyłębski A., *Hermeneutyczny zwrot filozofii* [Hermeneutic Turn of Philosophy], Wyd. Naukowe UAM, Poznan 2005.

Przyłębski A., *Historyzacja a priori – zdrada czy produktywna kontynuacja filozofii transcendentalnej Kanta*, in K. Śnieżyński (ed.), *Immanuel Kant i świat współczesny. W 200. rocznicę śmierci Immanuela Kanta*, Wydawnictwo Wydziału Teologicznego UAM, Poznan 2004.

Przyłębski A., *Nietzsche i hermeneutyka*, in R. Kozłowski, K.C. Cern (eds), *O filozofii Fryderyka Nietzschego*, Wyd. Naukowe UAM, Poznan 2006.

Przyłębski A. (ed.), *Język – Świat – Rozumienie*, Expol, Włocławek 2007.

Przyłębski A., *W poszukiwaniu królestwa filozofii. Z dziejów neokantyzmu badeńskiego*, Wyd. UAM, Poznan 1993.

Ricoeur P., *Oneself as Another*, transl. K. Blamey, University of Chicago Press, Chicago and London 1992.

Ricoeur P., *Refleksja dokonana. Autobiografia intelektualna*, transl. P. Bobkowska-Nastarzewska, Wyd. Antyk, Kęty 2005.

Ricoeur P., *Oneself as Another*, University of Chicago Press, Chicago and London 1994.

Rigobello A., "Heideggers Kritik des Begriffes »Wert« und die praktische Bedeutung von »Eigentlichkeit«," in D. Papenfuss, O. Pöggeler (eds), *Zur philosophischen Aktualität Heideggers*, Klostermann Verlag, Frankfurt am Main 1991, vol. 1.

Rorty R., *Etyka zasad a etyka wrażliwości*, transl. D. Arbiszewska, "Teksty Drugie" 2002, no. 1-2.

Schleiermacher F.D.E., *Kritische Gesamtausgabe*, Walter de Gruter, Berlin – New York 1980.

Schneider G.H., *Der tierische Wille. Systematische Darstellung und Erklärung der tierischen Triebe und deren Entstehung, Entwicklung und Verbreitung im Tierreich als Grundlage zu einer vergleichenden Willenslehre*, Leipzig 1880.

Scholtz G., *Ethik und Hermeneutik. Schleiermachers Grundlegung der Wissenschaften*, Suhrkamp Verlag, Frankfurt am Main 1995.

Schönherr-Mann H.-M., "Hermeneutik als Antwort auf die Krise der Ethik," in H.-M. Schönherr-Mann (ed.), *Hermeneutik als Ethik*, W. Fink Verlag, München 2004.

Schönherr-Mann H.-M., *Friedrich Nietzsche*, W. Fink Verlag, Paderborn 2008.

Searle's J., *Mind, Language and Society*, Basic Books 2008.

Stachewicz K., *Problem ugruntowania moralności. Studium z etyki fundamentalnej*, Wydawnictwo Naukowe Semper, Warsaw 2006.

Strzelecki R.: *Ethos i wolność. W poszukiwaniu etycznej wymowy* Bycia i czasu *Martina Heideggera*, Wydawnictwo Uniwersytetu Jagiellońskiego, Cracow 2006.

Tietz U., *Hans-Georg Gadamer zur Einführung*, Junius Verlag, Hamburg 1999.

Troeltsch E., *Religia, kultura, filozofia*, transl. A. Przyłębski, Wyd. Poznańskie, Poznan 2006.

Vattimo G., *La fine della modernità*, Garzanti Editore, Milano 1985; Polish translation – *Koniec nowoczesności*, trans. M. Surma-Gawłowska, Universitas, Cracow 2006.

Vattimo G., *Le avventure della differenza*, Garzanti Editore, Milano 1980.

Vattimo G., *The End of Modernity*, Johns Hopkins University Press, 1991.

Weber M., *"Duch" kapitalizmu"* [The Protestant Ethic and the Spirit of Capitalism], in Z. Krasnodębski, *M. Weber*, Wiedza Powszechna, Warsaw 1999.

Wittgenstein L., *Dociekania filozoficzne* [Philosophical Investigations], transl. B. Wolniewicz, Wydawnictwo Naukowe PWN, Warszawa 2000.

Wittgenstein L., *O pewności* [On Certainty] (note 220), transl. M. and W. Sady, Spacja, Warszawa 1993.

Wolicka E., *Rozważania wokół Kanta. Prolegomena do filozofii kultury jako krytyki władz podmiotu*, Towarzystwo Naukowe KUL, Lublin 2002.

Zimmermann R., *Moral als Macht. Eine Philosophie der historischen Erfahrung*, Rowohlt Verlag, Reinbek bei Hamburg 2008.

Index of persons

* References to footnotes are in italics.

Philosophie: Forschung und Wissenschaft

Assunta Verrone; Peter Nickl (Hg.)
Welche Gerechtigkeit?
Texte zum 4. Festival der Philosophie 2014
Bd. 45, 2016, 222 S., 24,90 €, br., ISBN 978-3-643-13315-1

Gaetano Chiurazzi; Davide Sisto; Søren Tinning (Eds.)
Philosophical Paths in the Public Sphere
Bd. 44, 2014, 288 S., 34,90 €, br., ISBN 978-3-643-90596-3

In-Suk Cha
Der Begriff des Gegenstandes in der Phänomenologie Edmund Husserls
Mit einem Geleitwort von Friedrich-Wilhelm von Herrmann
Bd. 43, 2. Aufl. 2014, 152 S., 49,90 €, br., ISBN 978-3-643-12555-2

María Elton Bulnes
Moral Science and Practical Reason in Thomas Aquinas
Bd. 42, 2013, 88 S., 29,90 €, br., ISBN 978-3-643-90417-1

Rainer Adolphi; Lutz Fricke (Hg.)
Identitäten des Selbst
Beiträge zu einem transdisziplinären Problemfeld
Bd. 41, 2017, 160 S., 24,90 €, br., ISBN 978-3-643-12362-2

Peter Nickl; Assunta Verrone (Hg.)
Wie viel Vernunft braucht der Mensch?
Texte zum 3. Festival der Philosophie Hannover 2012
Bd. 40, 2015, 180 S., 24,90 €, br., ISBN 978-3-643-12285-8

Christian Mueller-Goldingen
Bertrand Russell
Studien zu seinem philosophischen Werk
Bd. 39, 2013, 224 S., 29,90 €, br., ISBN 978-3-643-11928-5

Gerd Pohlenz
Zur Lage der Philosophie
Ihre verborgene historische Kontinuität und Zielperspektive
Bd. 38, 2012, 408 S., 39,90 €, br., ISBN 978-3-643-11723-6

Benedikt Fait; Daniela Zumpf (Hg.)
Identität Logik Kritik
Festschrift für Ulrich Pardey zum 65. Geburtstag
Bd. 37, 2014, 312 S., 34,90 €, br., ISBN 978-3-643-11303-0

Raimund Nowak; Assunta Verrone; Peter Nickl (Hg.)
Nachhaltigkeit denken
Texte zum 2. Festival der Philosophie Hannover 2010
Bd. 36, 2012, 200 S., 19,90 €, br., ISBN 978-3-643-11044-2

Robert Zimmer; Martin Morgenstern (Hg.)
Gespräche mit Hans Albert
Bd. 35, 2011, 176 S., 19,90 €, br., ISBN 978-3-643-10957-6

Gerd Pohlenz
‚Gewalttätigkeit' *und* ‚moralisches Motiv'?
Das Konzept zweier Weltaspekte als Auflösung eines geschichtswissenschaftlichen Dilemmas. Mit einem Epi(dia)log zu den drei Bänden 2007 – 2009
Bd. 34, 2009, 480 S., 29,90 €, br., ISBN 978-3-643-10471-7

LIT Verlag Berlin – Münster – Wien – Zürich – London
Auslieferung Deutschland / Österreich / Schweiz: siehe Impressumsseite

Paul Richard Blum
Das Wagnis, ein Mensch zu sein: Geschichte – Natur – Religion
Studien zur neuzeitlichen Philosophie
Bd. 31, 2010, 336 S., 39,90 €, br., ISBN 978-3-643-90032-6

Jean François Revel
Geschichte der westlichen Philosophie
Von Thales bis Kant. Übersetzt und eingeleitet von Gerd Lamsfuß-Buschmann
Bd. 30, 2010, 488 S., 59,90 €, br., ISBN 978-3-8258-1168-6

Karl-Heinz Delschen; Jochem Gieraths (Hg.)
Europa – Krise und Selbstverständigung
Kommentierte Schlüsseltexte aus dem philosophischen Feld von Nietzsche, Simmel, Heidegger, Gadamer, Derrida, Habermas u. a.
Bd. 29, 2009, 328 S., 29,90 €, br., ISBN 978-3-8258-1159-4

Gerd Pohlenz
Macht und Moral
Zum strukturellen Kontext der europäischen Geschichte des Geistes und der Politik
Bd. 28, 2008, 512 S., 29,90 €, br., ISBN 978-3-8258-1043-6

Wulf Kellerwessel
Regel und Handlungssubjekt in der gegenwärtigen Moralphilosophie
Kritische Studien zum Neo-Intuitionismus, Neo-Egoismus und Partikularismus
Bd. 27, 2006, 128 S., 14,90 €, br., ISBN 978-3-8258-0031-4

Melanie Obraz
Das schweigende Bild und die Aussagekraft des Rezipienten in Bezug auf ästhetische und ethische Werturteile
Grundlagen für eine phänomenologisch ausweisbare Kunstphilosophie
Bd. 26, 2006, 504 S., 34,90 €, br., ISBN 3-8258-9736-2

Gerd Pohlenz
‚Wert und Sinn': Prinzip der Realität und der Geschichte
Warum die Moderne und die Wissenschaften von der Antike einander brauchen
Bd. 25, 2007, 264 S., 17,90 €, br., ISBN 978-3-8258-9301-9

Yves Bizeul (Hg.)
Gewalt, Moral und Politik bei Eric Weil
Bd. 24, 2006, 192 S., 17,90 €, br., ISBN 3-8258-9218-2

Wulf Kellerwessel
Michael Walzers kommunitaristische Moralphilosophie
Kritische Analysen zu *Drei Wege in die Moralphilosophie*, *Moralischer Minimalismus* und *Zwei Arten des Universalismus*
Bd. 22, 2005, 144 S., 14,90 €, br., ISBN 3-8258-9090-2

Renate Dürr; Gunter Gebauer; Matthias Maring Hans-Peter Schütt(Hg.)
Pragmatisches Philosophieren
Festschrift für Hans Lenk
Bd. 20, 2005, 464 S., 39,90 €, br., ISBN 3-8258-7131-2

Kurt Salamun (Hg.)
Fundamentalismus „interdisziplinär"
Bd. 19, 2005, 360 S., 17,90 €, br., ISBN 3-8258-7621-7

LIT Verlag Berlin – Münster – Wien – Zürich – London
Auslieferung Deutschland / Österreich / Schweiz: siehe Impressumsseite